A JOURNEY IN LANGUAGES
AND CULTURES

A Journey in Languages and Cultures

The Life of a Bicultural Bilingual

François Grosjean

OXFORD
UNIVERSITY PRESS

OXFORD
UNIVERSITY PRESS

Great Clarendon Street, Oxford, OX2 6DP,
United Kingdom

Oxford University Press is a department of the University of Oxford.
It furthers the University's objective of excellence in research, scholarship,
and education by publishing worldwide. Oxford is a registered trade mark of
Oxford University Press in the UK and in certain other countries

First Edition published in 2019

Impression: 1

Published in the United States of America by Oxford University Press
198 Madison Avenue, New York, NY 10016, United States of America

British Library Cataloguing in Publication Data
Data available

Library of Congress Control Number: 2018964553

ISBN 978-0-19-875494-7

Printed and bound in Great Britain by
Clays Ltd, Elcograf S.p.A.

To Lysiane

Contents

Preface and Acknowledgments

Seen from afar, my linguistic and cultural life could be seen as very ordinary... and rather French, Parisian even. I was born in Paris to a French father, I have a very French name, I lived my early years in a little French village outside Paris, did my university studies at the Sorbonne, and got my first job at the Université de Paris 8. I even married my French wife of 50 years in Paris. And our first son was born in Paris. Who knows, I may even pass away in the city of lights and someone could then say that I had been a true Parisian who hadn't moved around that much.

But my life, as we will see, was not meant to be so straightforward, at least linguistically and culturally. I am bilingual in French and English, but changed language dominance four times in my life due to repeated migrations. I acquired other languages to varying degrees, including American Sign Language, but then lost them. And because I lived for long periods of time in different countries—France, Switzerland, England, and the United States—I am a mosaic of four cultures.

As this moving in and out of languages and of cultures took place—learning and then forgetting some languages, adapting to some cultures, and even rejecting one for a short while—I remained very conscious of what was taking place. My own life in languages and cultures, and my own reflections on what I was living through, played a major role in my scholarly work on bilingualism and biculturalism. I started studying what it means to live with two or more languages, in various cultures, when

I was a Master's student in Paris, more than fifty years ago, and have continued to do so to the present day. Of course, as a psycholinguist, I have used the tools of our trade—description, experimentation, modeling—to better understand who we are. But it is true that many of the views, concepts and models I have proposed as a scientist have been influenced by my own itinerary as a bilingual and bicultural person.

As I wrote in an earlier book,[1] living with several languages and in different cultures is not the burden or the problem that some make out, but neither is it the complete bliss that others would have us believe. Bilingualism and biculturalism are quite simply a fact of life for millions and millions of people, with their ups and down, their good times and their bad times, their moments of joy, and their moments of frustration.

Since the words "bilingual" and "bicultural" will be used frequently in what follows, it is important to give a brief definition of each from the start. I will then discuss these notions in more depth in the pages that follow. A bilingual is a person who uses two or more languages, or dialects, in everyday life. As for a bicultural person, he/she takes part, to varying degrees, in the life of two or more cultures, adapts, at least in part, his/her attitudes, behaviors, values, languages, etc. to cultural situations or contexts, and combines and blends features of the cultures involved.

This book could not have been possible without the encouragements I received from the famous British linguist, David Crystal. He had just read my *Bilingual: Life and Reality*[2] and he wrote to me to say that my own story, which I referred to from time to time in the book, would make for fascinating reading. He even told me who to write to—Oxford University Press. There, I made contact with an old acquaintance, Julia Steer, who had helped me in the latter stages of my book, *Studying Bilinguals*,[3] an overview of my research in the field covering some twenty-five years. She kindly asked me to send her a book project, and after having obtained the advice of outside reviewers, she gave me the go-ahead to start. Once the book was finished, she gave me many valuable editorial suggestions. So both David and Julia were instrumental in getting this book off the ground, and I wish to tell them how grateful I am to them.

My warmest thanks also go to Dr. Penny Boyes Braem, a longtime friend, whose comments on the manuscript I found very helpful, to Vicki Sunter (Senior Assistant Commissioning Editor), Lydia Shinoj (Senior Project Manager), as well as Andrew Woodard (copy-editor) and Michael Janes (proofreader).

One person—my wife, Lysiane—has been a witness for half a century to both my life as a bilingual/bicultural and that of the psycholinguist researching the phenomenon. She has accompanied me through good times and bad times, has been a wonderful sounding board for my ideas, and has herself been an example of bilingualism in action. I dedicate this book to her and thank her wholeheartedly for her presence and her support.

1
Roger and Sallie

I have often been asked whether my parents, Roger and Sallie, fostered my own bilingualism from birth, that is, made me a simultaneous bilingual, and the answer I give is they didn't. Neither of their families were known for their bilingualism with one exception. On my French father's side, life seemed to have been very monolingual all the way down to both his own father, Joseph Grosjean, a judge in Northern France, and his mother, Henriette Boudet-Cauquil, a stay-at-home mother. Since Henriette was originally from Montpellier, maybe her parents or grand-parents had spoken Occitan, along with French, but I have never found any evidence for this.

On my English mother's side, monolingualism was the norm as well. Francis Gordon Pratt, her father, a naval architect, knew some school French but not much more, and Ruth Shipway, her mother, may have done so too. There had been a period of bilingualism in the early 19th century on Francis's side, though, when his French ancestor, Henri Jean-Baptiste Victoire Fradelle, a historical painter and portraitist, moved from France to Italy for a few years, and then settled in England. Fradelle was trilingual—French, Italian, English—and his wife and he brought up their children bilingual in French and English.

A Journey in Languages and Cultures. First edition. François Grosjean.
© François Grosjean 2019. First published 2019 by Oxford University Press.

Fradelle had an interesting life in the world of fine art. Originally from Lille, he was a student at the Ecole des Beaux-Arts in Paris during the French Revolution. This is where, one day, he witnessed Marie-Antoinette being led to her execution on the Place de la Révolution, now known as the Place de la Concorde. It marked him deeply and several years later he did a very realistic painting of the scene which can be seen at the Conciergerie in Paris. Henri left for Italy in 1808 and started to specialize in the domains that were to make his reputation: religious, literary, and historical subjects. He probably met his future English wife there, and in 1816, he arrived in England where he lived, with the exception of a short return to France in the 1830s, until he died in 1865. His work was in demand for about twenty years and he exhibited his paintings at the British Institution and at the Royal Academy Summer Exhibition.

I remember my grandfather, Francis, telling me that Fradelle's daughter, Caroline, had spoken French to her son, Gustavus, his own father. However, that tradition died away and Francis's French was learned in school like that of other members of the gentry and was used quite infrequently, such as when he raced motor boats in Monte Carlo. As for Ruth's family, the Shipways, the only glimpse of bilingualism was that of her sister, Faith Shipway, who spent some time in a school in Belgium. She was then to marry a French general and became an active English–French bilingual.

How about my parents? Did Roger, a French Air Force fighter pilot at the time of my birth, and Sallie, an English theater stage manager, learn one another's language before they met? It would appear that Roger had learned some English in his boarding school, the Collège de Marcq en Baroeul, near Lille. When I looked at documents from his school days, I found that he had obtained a runner's-up prize in English translation and grammar at the age of 16. He probably didn't use the language much while at school, and probably not at all during his Air Force training in 1939 and then his stint as a pilot in France until 1942. As for Sallie, I have found no evidence that she learned French in her English boarding school which she left at age 13. If she had, it must have been very elementary. She then entered the equestrian world of show jumping and, later, stage managing in England, and didn't need a foreign language.

Roger reached England in 1943 and stayed there for a year as a member of the Free French Air Force. It was at that time that he was able to put to use the English he had learned in school. All the more so when he met my mother at the end of that year. They started to live together (I will come back to this in a later chapter) and when my father was posted to North Africa in July 1944, they wrote to one another in English. In a letter to Sallie, Roger expressed his frustration at not being able to express exactly what he wanted to say, and about the lack of depth he felt in a language he didn't know well: "Excuse me my English, but I'm writing without a dictionary. After a busy day, I'm too tired to look up the words that I need." And, "I am sad because I cannot tell you in English all the love I feel for you. My knowledge of it is so basic. Please learn French."

Sometimes, he would quite simply write in French but would nevertheless end in English to please Sallie. To give an idea of Roger's mastery of English, I am reproducing two short extracts below. The first, written just after his departure from England, tells Sallie to be careful now that she is several months pregnant with their first child, my sister:

"Darling, I am anxious to know how you are now, how you manage with 'Junior'. I should like tell you as before every minute: don't ride, don't raise heavy things, be careful your health, you must sleep and eat well and so on. (You know all!!)."

In the second extract, from a letter written five months later, he talks about receiving the news in late 1944 that their baby girl, Brigitte, is born (Sallie is still in England and Roger is now in Paris):

"We had a daughter. Really, darling, when I received today your wire, 'Sorry to disappoint you by a girl', I was not at all disappointed. I prefer now a daughter to a son. And you, are you disappointed?"

Clearly, Roger could make himself understood but, as to be expected, there were many interferences from French, that is, deviations from the language being written or spoken (in this case, English) stemming from the influence of the deactivated language (here, French). This is a frequent phenomenon in bilinguals, especially in their weaker language, and we will come back to it frequently.

Together in France

In March 1945, Sallie managed to obtain all the documents necessary to join Roger in Paris after his time in North Africa. For her, it was a major move, both linguistically and culturally. She noted in her autobiography, "I settled down to domestic life which amused me for a while, [as] it was all so new. Most of my time was spent in [food] queues, where I learned French and took cooking lessons!" In fact, she probably went through culture shock, in a country she didn't know and whose language she did not speak. Roger and Sallie spent a bit more than two years living together in Paris, before separating. They probably spoke either French or English together, depending on the context, the topic, the presence of others, etc. They also probably did a lot of language mixing to make sure the other understood what was being said. Both languages were present in their everyday lives and surroundings, French of course, but English also. For example, Sallie got hired as a stage manager by the Entertainments National Service Association (ENSA) which provided entertainment to British armed forces personnel. Since she worked in two Parisian theaters for them, the Théâtre Marigny and then the Théâtre de la Madeleine, she used both languages daily. In addition, Roger and Sallie had both French- and English-speaking friends during their time together.

Looking back on the linguistic and cultural situation that my parents were in just before I was born in 1946, I realize now that everything was set for them to bring me up bilingual from birth, but they didn't. For example, they could have used the one person–one language approach employed frequently by parents to make children bilingual from birth. Roger would have spoken to me in his mother tongue, French, as would his parents, friends, and various acquaintances. Sallie, on the other hand, would have used English. Since it would have been the weaker of the two languages, she could have found some support from English-speaking friends and maybe even English baby-sitters spending a year in Paris. It didn't happen for at least two reasons. First, the approach requires some organization and discipline, and neither of my parents seemed interested in pursuing it. They no longer got along, even though they'd only been together for such a short time. As my mother wrote later about that period, "A folding marriage that had never been was not a good basis on which to bring another child into the world."

The second reason I did not become a simultaneous bilingual is that consciously raising a bilingual child was not something one did as frequently then as one does now. I wonder if they even knew it was possible. It should be recalled that during the first half of the last century, bilingualism in children was perceived negatively. The words of the educator and linguist, Simon S. Laurie, were still often cited by doctors and other child care specialists: "If it were possible for a child or boy to live in two languages at once equally well, so much the worse. His intellectual and spiritual growth would not thereby be doubled but halved. Unity of mind and of character would have great difficulty in asserting itself in such circumstances."[1] Thus, as we will see in the next chapter, I started my life as a monolingual.

The evolution of their bilingualism

How did my parents evolve linguistically and culturally over the years after leaving one another? My father, the one who was the more bilingual of the two, reverted back to monolingualism when he separated from my mother in 1947. He no longer needed his English when he reoriented his career to French archeology, and he had no one to speak it to. It became rusty, he searched for his words, and I even remember him asking me to translate short things for him such as letters to English colleagues when I was in my teens. On the other hand, Sallie was just at the beginning of her journey in languages and cultures. First, her French improved greatly when she started working as a model for the *haute couture* creator, Jacques Griffe, in Paris. She stayed with him from 1948 to 1952. As a reporter for the Daily American Weekly wrote in 1961: "She became . . . his star model, with police escorts everywhere she went to protect her and the millions of dollars of jewelry she wore."

To maintain her ties to the equestrian world which she belonged to in England, Sallie would also go out to Maison Laffitte, the track near Paris, to help train race horses there. She also spent most of her leisure time at Café de Flore, in St. Germain des Prés, where she met her new partner, Jean-Jacques, a French-speaking Swiss, and where she had many friends. Thus, in the span of a few years, she went from being monolingual in English to being bilingual in English and French. Her French became very fluent but she continued speaking it with a strong English accent, having started so late.

Her journey in languages and cultures was not over however. During a short vacation in Stresa, Italy, in 1952, she met André, a rich French-Italian business man who fell madly in love with her. He proposed that she move to Italy to be with him and he bought her an apartment in Rome and a horse-breeding farm outside the city. Practically overnight, she left Paris and started a new life as a breeder and trainer. Of course, she had to learn Italian, which she did rapidly. "La Signora Pratt" as she was known (she had changed her name to Jill Shipway Pratt) built herself a fine reputation in Italy and abroad, and many of her horses were sold in France, England, and even the United States. She was one of the very first women trainers and breeders in Italy and was highly respected. Sallie was to spend the rest of her life there.

After her death in 2009, and because we had been estranged for so long, I went to visit people who had known her, and wrote to others I could not go and see. I wanted to know more about her life in Italy. My interlocutors and I didn't talk much about the linguistic and cultural aspects of her life, with one exception though. One of her longtime friends, Sophie Decrion, raised an issue that has intrigued many bilinguals, as well as researchers on bilingualism, over the years. She believed that Sallie could have different personalities, and that this came through when she changed languages. In French, she said, she was the top model with the outspokenness of an independent and unconventional woman. In English, her very classic and upper-class schooling came through; upbringing and horse racing were paramount. And in Italian, she was the diva, the star, surrounded by a flock of admirers whom she scorned, and by a few ordinary people as well as jockeys and lads whom she respected.

What can we say about this? It is clear that different contexts and domains trigger different attitudes, impressions, and behaviors in speakers. Just think of the way you speak with your best friend, and the behavior and personality you adapt with him or her, and think of how this changes in the most formal interactions you have, such as with a school head, religious authority, or employer. Bilinguals behave in a similar way, but with one difference. They have two or more languages they can use. Does this mean they change personality when they change language? I don't believe so. In my first book on bilingualism, *Life with Two Languages*, back in 1982, I reasoned that what is seen as a change in personality is simply a shift in attitudes and behaviors corresponding to a shift in situation or context, independent of language. Different situations make one behave differently, whether one is using one language or several languages. In other words, it is the environment and the interlocutors together that cause bilinguals to change attitudes, feelings, and behaviors (along with language)—and not their language as such.

2

My early monolingual years

was born on March 11, 1946, in a small birth clinic in the 7th arrondissement in Paris. My first year and a half was spent in my parents' apartment, rue Emile Allez in the 17th arrondissement. It was very small and, according to various people who visited my parents at the time, I used to sleep in a box either on top of a cupboard or out on the balcony, even when it was very cold.

My parents separated when I was just over one year old after many months of conflict between the two. The district court gave Sallie custody of my sister and me, and my father had visiting rights two Sundays a month. Since Sallie worked part-time as a theater stage manager, we were often under the care of part-time nannies or we stayed with friends for the day. At one point, I was taken by my father and lived with him for a month or two, and his own father, Joseph, in Gournay-sur-Marne, outside Paris. At the end of 1947, our mother put us in a foster home in Varennes-sur-Seine, some 53 miles east of Paris. The lady we stayed with for at least eighteen months, Madame Briare, clearly showed us a lot of affection. Many years later, I was to find two letters she had written to my father when Sallie removed us from her care in 1949. Here are a few extracts: "I'm so sad as I loved your children,

A Journey in Languages and Cultures. First edition. François Grosjean.
© François Grosjean 2019. First published 2019 by Oxford University Press.

and took care of them as if they had been my own ... I would love to have news of the children. You know, Monsieur Grosjean, I behaved with them as if they were my own children ... I would love to see my little François again as well as Brigitte." I have no recollection of Madame Briare or of our stay in Varennes, but I regret not having been able to visit her when I was an adult to thank her belatedly for her love.

Madame Wallard

Our life in a totally French environment was to continue for several more years as Sallie simply moved us to the other side of Paris and put us in a second foster home at Villiers-Adam, some 21 miles north-west of Paris. Madame Wallard had just lost her husband, an examining magistrate, and she had decided to look after a few children. She lived just outside the small village which, surprisingly, had been the object of a book in 1935, *Un village renaît*, detailing the urban renewal it had gone through. I remember my years there quite well and still marvel to this day that I had been a totally monolingual little boy, in a very typical French village, before becoming bilingual.

Madame Wallard lived some five minutes from the village center which had a small common on which had been built a rather large and not very attractive building in the preceding century. It combined the village mairie, the primary school, and the teachers' lodgings. Surrounding the common were a number of houses, some with stores. There was also a blacksmith's shop, and one or two farms. The 16th-century church wasn't far away.

Before being old enough to go to school, I stayed with Madame Wallard and any other children she might have had at the time. We played in the veranda and in the garden which led down to the main road. I often sat on a wall there and looked at the cars going by. I always hoped that one of them would stop and that either my father or my mother would get out and tell me it was time to go home. Madame Wallard was very kind to me but I realized very early on that I really should be somewhere else, with my parents, or at least one of them. Of course, they came to visit from time to time, but it wasn't the same as living with them. Concerning the language we used together during their rare visits, it was French with both; I don't ever remember my mother speaking English to either of us.

Madame Wallard had teenage grandsons who visited from time to time and it was always fun playing with them. Once I was old enough, I ran errands for her such as going to the local store in the village to get bread or anything else that was missing. And at around four in the afternoon, I'd be given a small milk can to get milk at the farm in the village. One day, I stopped off to play with other children, the can got pushed over and the milk spilt out. When I got home, Madame Wallard was mad at me and spanked me.

We'd often go and play in the nearby forest which had small mounds and cavities we could hide in. I learned later that the Germans had stockpiled their ammunitions there during the war and the allies had blown them up, hence the holes all over the place. The war was still quite present—it had stopped only seven years or so before—and one of the boys with Madame Wallard had a German father and a French mother whom I'd met. I didn't quite realize at the time what that must have meant for the two of them during the war years and the years immediately afterwards. And I still wonder how the boy lived with this later in his life. They were a beautiful couple—it was then that I became attracted to parents who were together as mine never were—and they seemed to love their little boy a lot. Whenever I think of the difficulties some bicultural couples may have, I think of them as an example of being very comfortable together despite their incompatible origins at the time.

Madame Wallard was so French, I realize now. She would call me "mon coco," talk to me as if I were a small adult, and be quite frank about certain things. Thus, one day she came into my room dressed to go out—I was in bed with some childhood illness—and she told me that she would be gone for about an hour and would soon be back. I asked her where she was going and she said that she'd be at the next-door neighbor's funeral. She added, off hand, that he had hung himself. I still remember, as I am writing this, that I shook with fear in my bed as I waited for her to come back.

The village had its yearly events that we would attend—the 14th of July (Bastille Day), of course, but also Armistice Day on November 11. And there was the Christmas Party offered to all the children by the mayor, Aristide Quillet, who was a well-known publisher in Paris specializing in dictionaries and encyclopedias. We put on our best clothes and were welcomed in his mansion outside the village to receive our presents. Another event that marked me was when, in the late fall, a distiller would bring his movable alembic and set up shop on the common. People would bring him their fruit and come back a day or two later for their eau-de-vie. I can still remember the pungent smell that hung over the common for days.

I started going to school when I was six, and recall having to wear a grey smock. I shared a desk with another child, there were two or three desks per row, and the teacher was at her desk in front of us. There was a huge map of France to her left—I spent so much time staring at it—and other maps to her right. We were taught to read and write on black slates and, when called upon, we would stand up next to our desk and reply. During breaks, we would go outside in the yard, all classes together, and run around.

Madame Wallard would help me with my homework when I got back from school and, after only a year, she made me write short letters to my parents to give them some of my news. Here is one that I wrote to my father in September 1953 when I was seven and a half (the translation is below):

"Mon cher papa. J'ai passé de bonnes vacances avec mes petits camarades et je me suis bien amusé. Je suis le meilleur coureur de ma compagnie. Maintenant je fais quelques devoirs de vacances. Viens me voir, papa, je serais très content. Ton petit garçon qui t'embrasse beaucoup. François Grosjean."

"My dear daddy, I had a good time during the holidays with my friends and I had lots of fun. I am the best runner of my group. I am now doing my homework for the holidays. Come and see me, daddy, I'd be so happy. Your little boy who gives you a big kiss. François Grosjean."

Abducted to Switzerland

My life as a monolingual, monocultural little boy in a small French village ended abruptly in December of that year when my mother arrived to take me out for the day, supposedly. In fact, we drove to Orly Airport where we took a plane to Geneva in Switzerland. When we arrived, we were met by André, her Franco-Italian friend who then accompanied us to a *home d'enfants*, a preschool boarding school, in Chesières, a little village in the Vaud mountains. There, I was reunited with my sister whom I had not seen for some time. It was only many years later that I learned that my parents' divorce had been finalized six months before and that my mother had obtained custody of both children. By abducting us out of French jurisdiction, she probably wanted to continue taking revenge on our father and make his visits to us difficult. It was certainly not due to her love for us as she often told my sister and me that she preferred animals to people, and notably to children.

I never heard from Madame Wallard again and it was only at the age of eighteen, when I was back in France for my university studies, that I returned to Villiers-Adam for a visit. The house was closed down and was looking quite decrepit. A neighbor told me that Madame Wallard had moved to Paris to spend her last years with her daughter. I passed by the school and, just on the off chance of meeting someone, I knocked on the door leading to the second year teacher's lodgings. My old primary school teacher opened the door and I introduced myself. He greeted me with much warmth and invited me in. Over coffee, we talked about those early years and he told me how pleased he was that one of his "boys" was going to university. As could be expected, the majority of my young friends had stayed in the village and had left school quite early on.

In Chesières, my life was not totally different from that in Villiers-Adam. I was with other children of my age, I shared a room with one or two, and elderly "tantes" (aunts) took care of us. In addition, the *home d'enfants* was French-speaking as was the environment. Of course, the scenery was totally different (Chesières and the neighboring Villars are beautifully situated in the Swiss Alps) and winter fun was sledding and skiing only a few yards from the school. A few weeks after my arrival, my maternal grandfather, Francis, came to visit us. He spoke French to us, to the best of his ability, and spent Christmas with us. I was to see quite a bit of him over the next ten years, mainly in

England, and he has a special place in my heart; he was so understanding, so very kind, and clearly thought about us a lot.

The "tantes" made sure we wrote to our father and here is a letter I probably dictated to them and then recopied with their changes in February 1954 (I was almost eight):

"Mon cher papa. J'ai bien reçu ta gentille lettre. Je t'en remercie beaucoup. Je vais très bien et fais beaucoup de ski. Jeudi nous sommes allés avec mes camarades à Bretaye—c'est une haute montagne où nous avons pu skier toute l'après-midi. Nous avons eu beaucoup de plaisir. Le restaurant où nous avons goûté était très joli. Je désire que tu m'apportes de Paris une grue. Je mange bien et je prends de belles couleurs. Je t'embrasse bien fort, mon cher papa, et à bientôt. François."

"My dear Daddy. I received your kind letter. Thank you for it. I'm very well and am skiing a lot. On Thursday, my friends and I went up to Bretaye; it's a high mountain where we skied the whole afternoon. We had a lot of fun. The restaurant where we snacked was very beautiful. I would like you to bring me a toy crane from Paris. I eat well and am looking healthy. I give you a big kiss, my dear Daddy; see you soon. François."

A few months later, Roger did come to visit, and did bring me a crane, but only stayed a few hours before continuing his trip down to Corsica to start his job there as an archeologist.

Just before Easter, one of the "tantes" told my sister and me that a man would come in once a week to give us English lessons as our mother had decided that we would attend English schools after the summer. The person who was himself Swiss was rather elderly and naturally only concentrated on oral speech, such as greetings, giving the time, saying simple things, etc. This was our first contact with English and it went quite smoothly. Things would speed up dramatically a few months later.

At the end of this monolingual period of my life, my French was the same as that of other boys my age. I had turned eight in March and was making progress in reading and writing. At that age, one doesn't yet master all the complexities of syntax nor all the subtleties of the morphology of a language like French. And, of course, one's vocabulary is still not very extensive. As for the pronunciation of sounds, it is normally in place. In my case, one sound was still not mastered and it was the local eye doctor whom I had gone to see for my near-sightedness who noticed this. He noted that I simply couldn't pronounce the sound /l/ as in "ballon" (ball). He tried to make me pronounce it over and over again, and I simply couldn't. I replaced it with the sound /n/, something that younger children sometimes did. Had I remained in a monolingual environment, I would have got over this last pronunciation hurdle after a few months. But moving over to English fossilized this problem which I have retained to this day. Interestingly, since the /l/ sounds are very different in the two languages, I don't have the same problem in English.

3

Becoming bilingual

I n the summer of 1954, someone came to transfer me from my *home d'enfants* to a small English school in the next village, Villars. It was temporarily in a large chalet before moving a few months later to an old hotel, the Hôtel Bristol. In the space of a few hours, I left my monolingual French world to enter an English-speaking world that was new to me. I have often asked myself why my mother had decided to send us to English schools when there were a number of French-speaking schools in the area. Was it to bring us even closer to her world, even though we didn't live with her, or simply to create more distance between our father and us? I've never fathomed it out. That said, I wouldn't be writing this book if this change of language had not occurred at that time. It led to so many other events in my life.

First steps in English

In my writings, I have talked of the problems met by language minority children on the first days of school in the majority language. They are often in a "submersion" or "sink or swim" mode, which can be particularly difficult if they do not understand or speak the language used in the school. They often feel

A Journey in Languages and Cultures. First edition. François Grosjean.
© François Grosjean 2019. First published 2019 by Oxford University Press.

lonely and insecure, especially if they are alone among children who already know the majority language, and their struggle is even harder when the teachers have no knowledge of their language and culture, not to mention being forbidden to use their own language among themselves. The testimonies of members of language minorities are numerous, and sometimes horrific, in the migration literature.

The situation I was in was far removed from this. Clearly, I went through a form of "submersion"—I was indeed dropped into a totally different language environment—but it took place softly and I don't remember suffering from it. First, my sister had accompanied me to the chalet and had stayed there for several weeks before joining her own school, Chatelard School, in Les Avants, Vaud. Thus, I could always try to figure out what was being said with her help. Second, many of the staff and some of the children knew some French and acted as translators when there was a need. Third, we were of course allowed to speak French, some of the personnel in the school were Swiss French (such as the main housekeeper, the cook, etc.), and the surrounding community was French-speaking. As a consequence, things could not have been better linguistically.

Aiglon was and has remained a very interesting school. Its founder, John Corlette, who was the head when I was there from 1954 to 1960, believed in a certain educational philosophy which he applied. For example, he put as much emphasis on the body as on the mind. He wanted students to be responsible, socially aware, and of service to others. In addition, it was important to show compassion, humility, and generosity, and be respectful of other ideas and opinions. Concerning physical development, students should have good living habits, exercise daily, and take care of themselves. They should accept challenges of all sorts—intellectual, academic, and in the domain of sports. Throughout my six years there, elements of this philosophy were applied with success, and still are today. It made our lives together so easy. And with the few boys at the time, it was literally like being in a large family—my very first.

My memory of my first years of school is of days punctuated with school work, long walks, a lot of sports (soccer, skiing, and skating), semi-official cultural activities, and less official sitting around playing or reading. The morning runs before breakfast, followed by a cold shower, and the meditation meetings just before classes are still firmly in my memory. It was always interesting to see who would lead the meditation (teachers took it in turn) and how they would fare; some were more relaxed about the whole thing than others. From time to time, the theme would actually wake us all up. One day, Mr. Corlette came in and gave us a pep talk on keeping the bathrooms clean. His "please aim straight" request is probably still engraved in all our memories.

When I started, we couldn't have been more than 30 boys or so, ranging from 8 to 18 years old. That meant that we did many activities together and only remained in our age groups for classes and in our bedrooms. Hence, I remember actually inter-acting with 16- and 17-year-olds quite naturally. For the first two years the boys were mainly British. By the time I left in early 1960, the school had grown quite a lot—it had moved down to Chesières in 1955—and the student population had become quite international with a large input of American students. That said, the vast expansion that was to take place in the late 60s and 70s had not yet occurred and the school was still not co-ed. Today it numbers some 365 boys and girls and is extremely well regarded, I am told.

Two new cultures

Aiglon was the place where I acquired English, making rapid progress and speaking like a native after only a few years. It was also the place where I came into contact with two new cultures, the British and the American. On the British front, I remember discovering the Beatrix Potter books, and reading aloud from them with the help of an elderly teacher, Mrs. Harding, who drank as much tea as she smoked. I then graduated to the adventures of Biggles and the Enid Blyton books. I was also captivated by tales of knights and sorcerers, and the alpine conquests of British mountaineers. And, of course, in history and geography classes, we mainly talked about Great Britain. From time to time, we would go to the British Ski Club cocktail in a nearby hotel where cups, for winners, and spoons, for runners up, were given after races organized by the club.

My sister and I also spent a few weeks from time to time with our grandfather, Francis, in England. He lived in Richmond, Surrey, and was still working, so during the day we would take care of ourselves and go for lunch at a little restaurant whose owner he knew. We spent a lot of time along the Thames, or wandering around the town. And when Francis was free, on weekends or during his own vacation time, he would take us to Kew Gardens, up to Hampton Court, or the Science Museum in Kensington where there were models of some of the yachts his firm, Cox & King,[1] had designed. We also went on longer trips such as to Wells, Somerset. Those stays did a lot to introduce us to the British way of life.

On the American front, most of my roommates were from the United States and were with their parents in Europe for a few years. They brought with them their language and culture, but also those little things that school boys enjoy such as comic books and Bazooka chewing-gum, angel fruit cake (sent by their parents), records of rock-and-roll singers, etc. One of my roommates was Casey Murrow, the son of the famous Ed Murrow, and I remember talking to him when we were in our room about America. I tried to imagine how big it was, how people lived there, the size of skyscrapers in the cities, the very cold winters and very hot summers, etc. Little by little I was permeated with American culture, and by the age of 12 or so, I certainly knew more about America than I knew about my home country, France, that I had left only four years before. I would dream of going to the States, never realizing that some sixteen years later I would indeed go there, and stay for twelve years.

Since my friends' parents knew that my own parents never came to take me out, they would invite me to join them for their outing with their son and sometimes even to spend a weekend with them. I loved it as it allowed me to get a taste of family life. Being in a family was so different from what I had known as a foster child and now as a boarder. I quickly became attached to the mothers who were so kind to me, and to the dads who would actually play with us, talk to us in a friendly manner, throw us a football outside, etc. Later, when I had my own young children, in the United States, I copied the American dad model I had observed as a young child.

When a roommate left for good with his parents, I inevitably felt sad as I had lost a friend and, via him, surrogate parents. I followed them in my mind on their trip back to the US via Paris, Le Havre, and then their whole week on some large transatlantic boat. But they didn't forget me, and several times, I would receive parcels with books, comic books, and candy. Starting age 11 or thereabouts, I started devouring American books for young boys and girls such as The Hardy Boys, Nancy Drew, etc. I would spend hours reading them and imagining the places described in the stories.

There were also members of the staff that I would get close to to make up for the absence of parents. One of them was Elizabeth, the school nurse. I still recall knocking on the door to her room and basically inviting myself in to spend some time with her. She loved musicals and would get me to listen to records she had brought back from England such as *The King and I*. I quickly learned that if I showed interest in a person, either a school mate or an adult, they would reciprocate and become friendly towards me. Much to my regret, Elizabeth left after two years, but more than 50 years later, through the school's magazine, I was able to link up with her again. I told her how much her presence and affection had meant to me at the time.

Thus, over my six years at Aiglon, through my daily contacts and conversations with boarders both from Great Britain and then, more and more, from the United States, my reading of children's books from those countries, my classes and inter-actions with British and American adults, I slowly acculturated into the British and American cultures. This didn't occur as it normally does in the countries in question, but high up in the mountains of Switzerland, in a boarding school.

Losing my French

As this was taking place, I was losing my French and my ties to my home country. While I continued to speak French outside the school—when we went skiing, for example, or in the local stores, or when I went to catechism at the local church—I rarely spoke it inside the school. I was excused from French classes which, with hindsight, was not such a good idea as they would have helped me stabilize and then improve my written French. The more my English improved, the more my French declined and fossilized. Not my simple conversational French, spoken without any accent, of course, but my written, more formal French. Below I reproduce two extracts from letters I wrote to my father when I was twelve, that is four years after my arrival in Aiglon (errors have been maintained; a translation is below each extract):

1. "S'il te plait, est-ce que tu pourras m'acheter pour Noël une petite radio qu'on marche avec du cristal; il sont toute petite et beaucoup de garçon sent on ici. Tu pourras l'envoyer ici. Nous avons commencé le ski. Les examait commence bientot."

"Please, could you buy me for Christmas a small radio that works with a crystal; they're very small and many boys have them here. You can send it here. We have begun to ski. Exams are starting soon."

2. "Je suis entrain de vous écrire en attendant les douches, c'on a le matin (froide) et le soir (chaude). Ici il a neigé et on a fait des forts de neige, mes la neige n'était pas assez bien pour le ski. Merci beaucoup pour la carte que j'ai reçue ce soir. A quoi cervais c'est tours que vous m'avez envoyer? Nous faisons beaucoup de travaille, et avec mon argent, je me suis acheter une vieille bicyclette. Elle marche bien."

"I'm writing to you while awaiting the showers that we have in the morning (cold) and the afternoon (hot). Here it has snowed and we have made snow forts, but the snow was not good enough for skiing. Many thanks for the card that I received this evening. What were those towers that you sent me used for? We work a lot, and with my money, I have bought myself an old bicycle. It works very well."

Those who know some French will recognize in the first extract the use of "qu'on marche" instead of "qu'on fait marcher," the wrong gender on the pronoun "il" after "radio," the problem with "sent on ici" instead of "en ont ici," the erroneous spelling of "examait" instead of "examens," etc. In the second extract, there are spelling problems ("c'on" instead of "qu'on," "mes" instead of "mais," "cervais" instead of "servaient," etc.), the use of the infinitive instead of the past participle, e.g. "m'avez envoyer" instead of "m'avez envoyé," "acheter" instead of "acheté," and so on. Clearly, a boy my age who had pursued his studies in French, would have made far fewer of these mistakes, if any of them.

As for my actual ties to France, I would go to Paris to see my father and his second wife, Jackie, every two years or so, for a week, or take a trip down to Montpellier to see my great-grandmother, and hence I got a taste of French life. But it simply was not enough for me to continue feeling at home there, much less to continue acculturating into the French culture.

Learning, using, and forgetting Italian

Surprising at it may be, I now had more ties with Italy than with France. My mother had moved there in 1952, and my sister and I would sometimes go there on vacation. Because of the fact that we spent most of our time on her horse farm, among its Italian-speaking employees, we started to acquire Italian by simply interacting with them. We didn't see much of our mother during the day as she would spend her mornings at the Rome racetrack and afternoons doing various other things, so we basically lived in an Italian environment. No one spoke our languages, English and French, and so we used Italian. The need for a language is one of the most important variables that accounts for its acquisition and, especially, its use. Sallie's right-hand man, Ettore, would often bring his wife and children down from Rome, and they stayed on the farm. So we also had children to play with and, of course, that was even better for acquiring the language.

As the years went by, my Italian became quite adequate, even though I spoke it with an English accent and not a French accent. This shows how quickly my language change had taken place at Aiglon and how English had become my dominant language. I never learned to read or write Italian but spoke it fairly fluently. My use of Italian continued for several years and lasted until my last trip to Italy, at age 16. I then no longer used it and, over the years, I slowly started to forget it.

It is worth saying a few words here about language attrition.[2] It is the flip side of language acquisition and is just as interesting linguistically, but attitudes towards it are very different. One often hears, "How wonderful you are learning language X" but how many times do you hear someone say, "How wonderful you are losing language Y." The process of language forgetting begins when the domains of use of a language are considerably reduced, if not simply absent, as was my case starting at age 16 with Italian. It lasts longer the older you are and is marked by hesitant language production as the speaker searches for appropriate words or expressions. There will also be frequent intermingling of languages as he or she calls on the dominant language, or other languages, for help. This happened to me when the Spanish I acquired as a student over a single year interfered greatly with my Italian, and still does. Pronunciation is also marked increasingly by the other language (or another language if there are several) and "odd" syntactic structures or expressions are borrowed from the dominant language.

Language comprehension is less affected, although the person may not know new words and new colloquialisms in the language that is being forgotten. People who are in an extended process of forgetting a language, as I still am with Italian, avoid using it because they no longer feel sure about it and they do not want to make too many mistakes. If they do have to use it, they may cut short a conversation so as not to have to show openly how far the attrition has progressed.

After six years at Aiglon, my mother wrote to me one day to tell me that I would go to another school the following term, this one in England. I was surprised, especially as the reason she gave me was that Aiglon was not sufficiently strict and that I needed to get a gentleman's education. Aiglon had become a family where I had found a few substitute parents. I had been there the longest, along with a friend Chris, and I was happy there. I now had to leave and it made me feel miserable.

I had arrived at Aiglon a little French boy who knew no English. I left six years later an English-French bilingual, with more ties to British and American cultures than to my original French culture. How would things evolve in a more traditional English boarding school?

4
Culture shock

I arrived in England in the spring of 1960 and was greeted at the train station by my mother's sister, Sheila, who lived with her second husband—she would have five in the end—on a small horse farm. She was my contact in England for the next four years as neither my parents ever visited me there. Basically, she helped me prepare the clothes, including the uniform, that I needed, and she dropped me off at school at the beginning of each term. Sometimes she invited me out for the day, or even for part of my vacations, but never more than a few days. Sheila was a member of the country gentry that would get together for fox hunts, among other activities. She was friendly towards me but I didn't find in her the surrogate parent I dreamed of.

Ratcliffe College

My boarding school, Ratcliffe College, was Catholic and was run by the Rosminians. It was situated outside Leicester and, at the time, it had about 300 boys, aged from 14 to 18. Very few came from abroad—we must have been five or so—and we, the foreigners, were expected to fit in quickly and without any fuss. England was still several decades away from being open to multiculturalism,

A Journey in Languages and Cultures. First edition. François Grosjean.
© François Grosjean 2019. First published 2019 by Oxford University Press.

and other cultures were frowned upon, especially those that had been unfriendly during the war. I was a frog, a representative of a nation that had given in to Germany and had collaborated with them. I would object and explain that my father had come over as a pilot to help the British war effort but it didn't help. Being French was definitely not a plus at that time. Even my name sounded odd and very quickly I was called "Frank" by both the staff and the students.

Ratcliffe was so very different from Aiglon that I literally went through culture shock during my first terms. The forms were kept separate and you simply did not communicate with the boys in forms above or below. The prefects had quite a bit of power and did not hesitate to admonish you or even punish you if you were caught breaking the rules. We slept in dormitories in the lower forms and in my first dormitory, there were some fifty beds. In my first term, I was placed in a form that was too difficult for me and I struggled. There were some subjects that I had not studied at Aiglon such as Latin and Physics, and so my end of term report was not very good. I was kept back which was not a long-term problem as I graduated at 18, like the other boys of my class. But at the time, I was quite embarrassed.

The boys were mainly from the Midlands and few had been abroad. When I told them about my life at Aiglon, with boys of different nationalities, skiing in the winter, the mixing of age groups, etc. they were surprised. I made the mistake of even telling them that with the older boys, we would sometimes take a walk towards the girls' schools to see if we could meet any. Some then went off and reported to the form master that I was telling tall stories. This was put in my end of term report, and I was then punished physically by my mother when I next went to Italy.

The school had corporal punishment which was triggered by getting a "note" from a teacher. How it was labeled mattered a lot. If it said, "Please punish X," then it meant you would get four hits with a cane; if "severely" was added at the end, then you would get six hits. I received two notes during my time at Ratcliffe, one because I was scratching my initials on top of my desk—it contained at least ten other signatures from preceding years—and once because I had not worked hard enough, supposedly. The scenario was as follows. You took the note down to the discipline master who then asked you to kneel, with your backside prominent and your head in front of your knees covered with your hands. He then took a billiard cane and struck you hard. He was not allowed to raise his arm above his shoulder but he could take a few strides to gather some momentum. Once the punishment was over, you thanked him and shook his hand. You then left his office and were greeted by a few friends who were there to cheer you up a bit. Of course, you were not supposed to cry, even though you wanted to. Much to my regret, I have never been able to cry since then, whether from pain or from joy.

Little by little, I managed to fit in as best I could. I did a sport, running, that did not require years of prior learning such as cricket or rugby. I joined the College Cadet Force and trained once a week with them. I took part in various school activities such as debating, and tried to be a good practicing Catholic although I was starting to have doubts. We were encouraged to go to mass every morning, high mass on Sunday being compulsory, as was saying the rosary all together on Saturday.

On the language front, I quickly lost the mid-Atlantic accent that I had acquired at Aiglon, surrounded as I had been by British and American friends, and became a Received Pronunciation (RP) speaker. My written English improved greatly with all the essays as well as précis writing that we did. The latter exercise, which I hated at the time, forced me to see what was essential in a text and to express it in far fewer words than in the original. It was a skill that I was to use for the rest of my life. Many years later, when I gave an interview concerning my *Psychology Today* blog on bilingualism, this is what I wrote:[1] "I love the challenge of having only 800–1000 words to present, as clearly as possible, the very essence of a topic and I thank belatedly my English teachers during my youth in England who made us do "précis" exercises each week. I didn't like them at the time but they have proved to be extremely useful when you have to summarize two or three scholarly papers in such a small space."

Continuing to lose my French

Within a strict British public school mold, there was little room for my French side, and so I played it down as best I could. I did have to take French classes though and realized that I was not as good as some of my classmates in grammar and translation. I had not learned the grammar of French explicitly, nor the translation equivalents of words using vocabulary cards, and I didn't write French very well. In many ways, I resembled the heritage language teenagers, as they are known today, in countries like the United States. Because the heritage language is usually their first language, these bilinguals often have little or no accent in that language. The advantages are many but there are also some disadvantages, such as that people expect you to know the language fluently as well as the culture that goes with it. Heritage language bilinguals become literate in their school language but less often in their first language. And even if they do learn to read and write their heritage language such as when they take it as a subject in school, the level reached may not be the same as with their second, dominant language.

Also, the domains of use of the heritage language may be limited (e.g. home, family, and some friends), and these bilinguals may not know the vocabulary of more specialized domains. Heritage language speakers may not be fully bicultural. Of course, they know a lot more about their heritage culture than, say, someone who is learning the language and culture for the first time in school. But there will be times when they may be surprised by certain behaviors and attitudes in their first culture. All of this applied to me when I was in Great Britain.

Our teacher of French spoke the language with a rather strong English accent and I must admit that I was surprised by this at first. I was still under the wrong impression that to be bilingual meant speaking your languages without an accent, which happened to be my case. I expected language teachers to be like that. In fact, I was to discover later that having a "foreign" accent in one or more languages is, in fact, the norm for bilinguals; not having one is the exception. There is no relationship between one's knowledge of a language and whether one has an accent in it.[2] During my last years at Ratcliffe, I was to study the work of Joseph Conrad, one of English literature's great authors, and I now wish someone had pointed out that he was trilingual in Polish, his native language, French, and English, and that he had a very strong Polish accent in English, his third language. But this didn't stop him from writing such outstanding prose in it.

As for foreign language teachers, it was many years later that I started to understand their special bilingual status.[3] They usually have insights into the linguistics of the language that regular bilinguals simply do not have. Any normal bilingual who has replaced a language teacher knows first-hand how difficult it is to suddenly explain a complicated aspect of a language that she usually speaks without giving it a thought. Language teachers are also used to translating and have available the translation equivalents of words that regular bilinguals do not always have. In addition, they are usually true admirers of the second language they teach—at least of its standard variety—and have a real love for its culture(s). When they convey this passion to their students, some become fascinated in turn.

Throughout my years at Ratcliffe, the question of where I would spend my vacations always arose. My mother was often too busy, or didn't want me in Rome. So, quite early on, she asked my aunt to find me a family where I could be a paying guest. That is how I came to know the Mooney family in Gerrards Cross. It was the first time that I lived in a family with two parents and a number of children, and very quickly I felt at home with them. The father was rather reserved but the mother, Mrs. Mooney, was particularly friendly and maternal. She was truly interested in my life, past and present, and we spent a lot of time talking about it. Very quickly, I forgot my guest status and I basically became the fifth child of the family. Since I was the oldest—the age of the others ranged from 5 to 13—I was always shown as the "example" to follow, someone who was serious-minded but also ready to take part in the life of the family. For the four years I was at Ratcliffe, I spent a lot of time with the Mooneys, whole vacations or several weeks here and there. I will remain forever grateful to them for the warm welcome they gave me and for their understanding.

A better ending

Although being a foreigner in an English public school in the early sixties was not easy, I found some compensation by doing well in my studies. I obtained eight GCE O levels, four in sciences (including Additional Mathematics) and four in arts. I could have gone the science route afterwards but for reasons that were never explained to me, I was guided towards the arts. This said, I maintained my interest in the sciences and after my university studies, found my vocation in experimental psychology which requires good knowledge of tools such as statistics, computer programming, and modeling. I prepared three subjects in the sixth form—English, History, and French—for each of which I obtained a first prize my last year. I also did a General Paper, and obtained A levels in all these subjects at the end of my stay.

As I was doing all of this, three out-of-class activities prepared me for later academic life. The first was taking part in the debating society where we were arbitrarily put on the side supporting or opposing a resolution such as, "This House Favors the Death Penalty." Having to defend views that you do not support, having to persuade the public that your points are valid, and having to listen to opposing perspectives and argue against them, were all extremely valuable. I am convinced that in my later life, my willingness to listen to different viewpoints, and to find compromise solutions, had its source in these debates.

The other outside activity that I did in my spare time was to read about, and around, historical events, literary works, and theories. Putting things in perspective, and anchoring them in their time and place, required extra work but allowed me to really know a topic. We did a bit of background research in class, but I did much more on my own, under the guidance of my teachers who were only too pleased to give me some extra readings. This allowed me to situate a work, or theory, or event, in its context and to understand it more fully. It was a very valuable asset that served me well in my future profession.

The third activity was quite different, it was cross-country running. Until my senior year, I did a lot of running and was a member of the cross-country team. I found each race difficult but I was encouraged to do my very best, notably by the coach, Father Fox, and to never give up. I believe that this training in endurance has had an impact on my life and has allowed me to never, or rarely, give up.

Since I was a bit of a rebel, I never made it to prefect or to a rank higher than corporal in the College Cadet Force. My very real problem, however, was that I was very lonely—I rarely saw my parents and had no real ties with them—and I no longer had those substitute parents I had found at Aiglon. After a couple of years, I turned to a priest, Father Wood, who took me under his wing and spent many hours talking to me. He too was slightly rebellious and understood perfectly what I was going through. As I was to write in my *Bilingual: Life and Reality* many years later, "As bilingual children and adolescents grow older, they must be allowed to talk about what it means to be bilingual and bicultural and to express some of the difficulties they may be having. Caring and informed adults must accompany them...and ease their passage from one stage to the next."[4] Father Wood was one of those and I owe him a lot.

In my lower sixth form, I received a letter from my mother to inform me that she would no longer continue paying for my education in England after my A levels. She told me to ask my father to finance my university studies. This came as a shock since she still had custody of both my sister and me, and had paid for our schooling up till then. In addition, being a foreigner in England, I knew that I couldn't get a scholarship. And so I wrote to my father to ask him for his help. He replied that he could indeed help me but that I had to come to Paris as university studies were less expensive there. So I gave up trying to get into either Oxford or Cambridge, although my grades made me a good candidate for either, and fell back on the Sorbonne. By the age of 18, I was much more British than I was French, and my dream universities, like those of my friends, were situated in England, not in France. My early disappointment was finally erased when, forty years later, I was invited to Oxford as a guest lecturer for a term.

I left Ratcliffe in early July 1964 after four years which had started off with difficulty but had ended normally thanks to my success in my studies, and to the teachers who had encouraged me. I had also made some good friends amongst the boys, some of whom—Brian, Iain, Francis, Michael—I was to keep in touch with over the years and see regularly.

Many years later, I received a letter from the Ratcliffe College Foundation telling me that they had created a pathway of granite stones leading to the new Preparatory School, and that they had dedicated a stone to me, "François Grosjean (64)—Psycholinguist." It was to honor me as a successful former pupil, and was to be a permanent reminder of my connection to Ratcliffe. I still have to go and see it, but I am pleased my old school had thought of me.

5
Returning to my first culture

A radical change in language need

In the span of a day—the time it took to go from England to France at that time—my need for each of my two languages changed dramatically. Suddenly, English was restricted to a few friends who came to see me in Paris, some letter writing, and parts of my university studies. French, on the other hand, became my most needed language after having been more or less dormant for some ten years. Even though I spoke French without an accent, with the exception of putting stress on nouns and verbs as one does in English, it was restricted in terms of lexical and grammatical knowledge, as well as language repertoires. In addition, I didn't write French very well, certainly not like my 18-year-old French peers who had just passed their *baccalauréat* and were entering university.

The predicament I found myself in can be explained quite simply by what I have termed the Complementarity Principle, that is, that bilinguals usually acquire and use their languages for different purposes, in different domains of life, with different people. Different aspects of life often require different languages.[1] If we were to take a bilingual's domains of language use, such as

A Journey in Languages and Cultures. First edition. François Grosjean.
© François Grosjean 2019. First published 2019 by Oxford University Press.

immediate family, distant relatives, work, sports, religion, school, shopping, friends, going out, hobbies, etc., and if we were to attach languages to these domains, we would see that some domains are covered by one language, some others by another language, and some by several languages. Rarely do bilinguals have all domains covered by all their languages.

Up until then, most of my domains were covered by English exclusively, but quite suddenly I had to use French in many of them, and I found this to be a frustrating experience. I tended to hesitate and fumble for words. I was often tempted to switch over to English for a word or a sentence, but this only worked when I was speaking with people who knew the language and didn't mind my mixing. I even reverted to borrowing words from English, i.e. pronouncing them like French words and integrating them into the sentence morphologically and grammatically, and then explaining them if I saw my interlocutor's eyes glaze over. Over the next few years, as my fluency in French picked up and it became my regular language, my language dominance changed and I slowly became a French-dominant bilingual. I simply couldn't have realized then that I would change dominance two more times before stabilizing my languages in my later years.

On the social and cultural levels, my adjustment to life in France was extremely painful. I suddenly realized that I belonged to neither culture. I was, and had always been, a stranger in England, but I had also become a stranger in France. There were so many things I simply didn't know about my home country. Those who didn't know me but who had in front of them a young man called "François Grosjean" who spoke French apparently fluently took it for granted that I shared their cultural knowledge. I wasn't a foreigner to whom you have to explain everything from A to Z, and whose mistakes and errors in adjustment you tolerate; and yet I wasn't like everyone else who had lived in France all of their lives. I knew little about French customs and habits, how people interacted, what was expected of me, and what surprised people. I was, in a word, a rare bird, and most people just did not know how to interact with me.

I was stumped by some very simple things, such as who had won the French National Football Championship that year, who the TV personality, Leon Zitrone, was, why there was a problem with the "pieds noirs" (the French who had lived in Algeria and who came back when the country became independent), and so on. Very simple things were often a mystery to me. For example, I remember going into a cinema a few weeks after my arrival and being shown to my seat by an attendant. I thanked her but she stayed there, and I suddenly realized she was expecting a tip. I blushed, found some change, and gave it to her. Later, I reflected that tipping was so very different from one country to the next and since then I have been extremely careful to do the right thing.

Who was I?

I found "my" people extremely distant, unfriendly, uninviting, and I suffered from the fact that they did not know how to situate me. But I too was undecided on who I was. Many years later, when I wrote my first theoretical paper on biculturalism which I will come back to in a later chapter, I noted that biculturals have to come to terms with their identity. They have to take into account how they are perceived by members of each of their cultures who base themselves on such factors as kinship, language, physical appearance, nationality, education, attitudes, and so on. The outcome may be similar (X is judged to be a member of culture A by all concerned) or contradictory (X is seen as belonging to culture A by members of culture B and to culture B by members of culture A). Rarely do biculturals receive the message that they are *both* A *and* B.

Faced with this double categorization, biculturals have to reach a decision as to their own cultural identity. They take into account how they are perceived and they bring in other factors such as their personal history, their identity needs, their knowledge of the languages and cultures involved, the country they live in, and so on. The possible outcomes are to identify solely with culture A, solely with culture B, with neither culture A nor culture B, or with both culture A and culture B.

I should have chosen the last alternative, i.e. that I was a member of both culture A and culture B, but I opted rather, at least for the first few years after my return to France, to be French only and to reject my English side. This was not a satisfactory solution in the long run as I had roots in both cultures, but it was my way of overcoming the difficulties of adapting, or readapting, to my home country. For a long time I felt that it was impossible to be bicultural—that it was too painful—and I therefore strove hard to belong to just one culture. Had the circumstances been different and had I been helped by my family and people who knew about these things when I first came back to France, life would have been easier and I could perhaps have identified with both cultures immediately. My final acceptance of my different cultures, to which I was to add the American and Swiss cultures, only came later.

I realize now that I was not the only one who had difficulties identifying with both cultures and admitting that one is indeed bicultural. The Franco-British journalist and writer, Olivier Todd, spent most of his life searching for his dual French and

English identity after philosopher and writer Jean-Paul Sartre told him that his problem was that he was divided between England and France. I had the pleasure of sitting down with Olivier Todd about ten years ago, after he published his auto-biography, *Carte d'identités*,[2] and I asked him about his biculturalism. I stressed the fact that one could be both A and B even if one culture is dominant. After a long silence he admitted that I was right and that he was indeed bicultural, although he was reluctant to adopt that term.

The Sorbonne

I enrolled at the Sorbonne in September 1964 in the first year *propédeutique* program in the "Certificat d'études littéraires générales." We had to take three subjects; one was compulsory, it was French, and the other two could be chosen. I chose English and History telling myself that if I worked on the same subjects as I had done for my A levels, things would be a bit easier. But this turned out to be only partly true as I had a lot of catching up to do. I had to greatly improve my written French, learn how to write essays in that language—they are structured very differently from their English counterparts—and I had to increase my knowledge of French literature. I also had huge gaps in French history as I had only studied English history and not its French counterpart. Knowing that I had to pass that first year in order to have access to the second year, I set myself a harsh work schedule. I forced myself to work ten hours a day, seven days a week. Time off to eat, go to courses or simply rest would not count in those hours. I undertook a heavy reading program in both French literature and French history which included not only the set readings but also general works that would give me the background

I needed to understand them. In order to change settings and to see people—sitting in my room for hours on end studying was a lonely affair—I would often go to the Bibliothèque Sainte-Geneviève, opposite the Panthéon, or to the Bibliothèque de la Sorbonne, both of which have lovely reading rooms.

That first year was probably the most difficult in my life. I no longer had the security of a boarding school, I lived alone in a room in my French grandfather's apartment whilst he was in a nursing home, and I hardly knew anybody. I would sometimes go to dinner at my father's place but I never stayed very long as I didn't feel comfortable in his presence. I had spent my life up till then either in foster homes or boarding schools and had never had the opportunity to develop a normal father–son relationship with him. As for my mother, she lived in Italy and had been inimical towards me during my youth, so at age sixteen I had broken off all ties with her.

Not everything was somber, however, as some of my English friends came over to see me. And I did meet other students in classes. I was surprised though that there were so few men in them. I had grown up in boys-only schools and simply didn't know how to interact with girls. I remained in my corner, therefore, and didn't say much. Several years later, I met one of those female students who told me that several of them had wanted to become friends with me but that I was so shy that they had given up, and had left me alone. I was less introverted with teachers since my Anglo-American schooling had encouraged me to ask questions in class, and discuss with teachers outside classes. I carried this habit over to my university lectures at the Sorbonne and it allowed me to get to know a few lecturers.

In the spring of 1965, I left my grandfather's apartment to move into a very small studio my father had bought in the heart of the Quartier Latin. My stepmother, Jackie, with whom I got along very well, had insisted that I have my own lodging. It was at 6, rue Christine, a narrow street that leads onto rue Dauphine, which itself leads onto the Pont Neuf. It was ideally situated for a student at the Sorbonne and I was to live there for the next seven years. The studio was on the very top floor, opposite that of a neighbor, Jackie, who had a 14-year-old son, Olivier. Over time, we became friends and she would invite me to dinner on Sundays when Olivier visited her (he lived the rest of the week with his father). She was the very first French person to bring me into their home, not counting my father, and I remain grateful to her to this day. I knew I could count on her whenever I needed to and, in turn, I collected her mail when she was absent.

The harsh work schedule I had given myself for that first year paid off and I passed my *propédeutique* exams in June, much to my surprise. Before continuing the degree program in English, I had several months of vacation, and I decided to hitch-hike across Europe and do a workcamp in Switzerland. Hitch-hiking was still something one did at that time and those who didn't have the means to travel would often resort to this mode of transportation. The important thing was to put yourself at a place where a car could stop and pick you up. It was also important to indicate your destination by being on the right road. And once picked up, it was crucial to be a good conversationalist as drivers often wanted someone to talk to. That first summer, I travelled many thousands of kilometers across various countries in Europe, staying at youth hostels along the way.

I had seen other hitch-hikers put flags on their backpacks and I did the same. However, to show how much a foreigner I was in my own country, I attached the flag with the red part on the left and the blue part on the right. I seemed to remember that in England I had seen somewhere that the French flag was red, white and blue. Of course, if I had heard "bleu, blanc, rouge" more often, I wouldn't have made the mistake. One driver actually commented on it saying he wasn't quite sure if I was French as the flag had been placed the wrong way round. I remained silent as I didn't want to go into the details of my past life.

The work camp was organized by the SCI (Service Civil International) in a small village, Andiast, in Graubunden in Switzerland. We were some 25 students from many different countries and our job was to build a small road, under the supervision of a road builder, leading to a pasture ground. The atmosphere was very friendly and it was a wonderful break from my monasterial life in Paris. I spoke more in one day than I had in one month that previous year.

The next two years at the Sorbonne leading up to the "licence" (Bachelor) went relatively smoothly. The program for English involved four certificates, two per year: English Philology with Old English, phonetics and linguistics; English literature; American civilization and literature; and Practical Studies in English. Of the four, I especially liked the first one which introduced me to the language sciences and opened up the path to my future career, not that I realized it at the time. Two professors made a big impression on me. The first one, Lionel Guierre, taught the phonetics course and introduced us to word stress rules in English. He used a computer and a large database to discover them, and it was the first time I heard about the use of computers in the language sciences. I was to be an adept of them later on. Guierre was extremely methodical and clear in his lectures and was a favorite of most students.

Antoine Culioli

The other professor, Antoine Culioli, who was to play an important role at the start of my career, was very different. He was very much a theoretical linguist and was just beginning to develop his Theory of Enunciative Operations. It was far from clear for us second-year students and many struggled to understand its main characteristics. My English schooling had encouraged me to really understand what was being said in courses, hence my frustration at the opacity of some of the things he proposed. I noticed however that my French peers were not put off, not that they understood more than me, but they were satisfied with getting the gist. Even today, I am sometimes amazed, and frustrated, by French intellectuals who produce rather impenetrable discourse which I don't fully understand. It must be my pragmatic English side coming through.

Antoine Culioli was clearly an up-and-coming star back in the 60s and his career was indeed going to be stellar in French academia. I was one of a few who got to know him a bit, something that was very rare as he was a rather reserved person. In addition, in those days, students hardly ever got to know their professors, at least until they reached the doctoral level, if that. When my father published his book, *La Corse avant l'Histoire*, in 1966, he gave me a copy for Culioli since it contained a poem in Corsican by his ancestor, Ghjuvan'Andria Culioli. So one day, after a lecture, I brought him the book and he thanked me. He then looked at the poem, and almost immediately pointed out an error... admittedly with a smile. Culioli, a Corsican brought up in Marseille, knew that my father was an archeologist in Corsica and he appreciated his discoveries, most notably those at Filitosa.

The other reason Culioli had noticed me is that he was always looking for native speakers of English in his audience whom he could call upon when discussing a difficult grammatical construction. This is how I describe such moments in my, "On becoming a psycholinguist," which I wrote for the Linguist List in 2012:[3]

"When I think about my first linguistics course, my mind wanders back to a large lecture hall in the mid-sixties at the University of Paris. Around 300 of us were attending a lecture on English Linguistics taught by Antoine Culioli. Suddenly, in his quiet voice, Culioli asked, 'Is François Grosjean there?'. I raised my hand and he continued, 'Tell me, in British English, would you say...(X)...or would you say...(Y)...?'. Because of my secondary schooling in England, I was one of the (quasi) native speakers that lecturers would call upon as linguistic informants. I don't remember the two alternatives Culioli gave me but I believe they concerned some very subtle difference in the use of a preposition. With 299 pairs of eyes looking at me, and not really seeing how the two alternatives diverged, I ventured, 'The former, I think!'. Culioli nodded his head and replied, 'Yes, that's what I thought'. He continued his lecture and I sat back and breathed a sigh of relief. Since then, I have the greatest respect for people who are informants!"

Both Lionel Guierre and Antoine Culioli were involved in administering the newly founded language lab where students could practice their pronunciation skills in individual booths. This was rather revolutionary at the time as having a good mastery of oral skills in a foreign language had simply not been given the importance it should have. The lab had a master console where a teacher could listen in on each booth and make suggestions on how best to pronounce individual sounds in words, or put the right intonation and stress on continuous sentences. Advanced students who were either native speakers of English or fluent bilinguals were taken on as tutors and, after a few weeks of training, were put in charge of sessions. That is the way I found myself in front of students for the first time at the age of 20. We had the title of "moniteur" and were given a small stipend for the work we did. Never did I realize at that time that this was the beginning of a long career in academia in three different countries.

Each of the four certificates I took ended with a set of written and oral exams, and everything went well until I hit the one that contained a translation from English into French. We were given a poem by William Wordsworth to translate and I struggled with it since I simply didn't have the equivalent language of poetry in French. Even though I had been back for three years, there were still some domains that were covered by English and not French. So I failed that exam in June and had to retake it in October, this time with success. It made me realize, once again, that the fact that I had missed ten years of French language and literature education during my adolescence continued to have an impact on my university studies.

A Master's thesis on bilingualism

Many students who obtained their "licence" (Bachelor) continued on to the "maîtrise" (Master) as it would allow them to prepare to be a secondary school teacher or to go on to doctoral studies. So I enrolled in the program and teamed up with an older student, Dounia Fourescot-Barnett, to work on my Master's thesis. I had met Dounia in one of our courses and had found her particularly friendly and even motherly. She would sit with another older student, Francine Oren, and I remember chatting with them about our Anglo-American ties. Dounia was married to a British businessman in Paris, and Francine to an American university professor. I believe it is Dounia who asked me if I would be willing to do a joint Master's thesis with her, and I agreed. I still felt insecure about my written French and I told myself that thanks to her, our thesis would be correctly written.

I told Dounia that I wanted to work on bilingualism in order to find out more about the topic and, indirectly, better understand what I was going through linguistically. She agreed as she too lived in a bilingual environment. In addition, she knew a number of bilinguals in Paris which would come in useful in our work. This was to be my first foray into the study of bilingualism, and was also my first team project, one of many in the years to come. We went to see Antoine Culioli and asked him if we could do a joint project on French–English bilinguals in Paris. He agreed under the condition that the final thesis be divided up into two parts, each one with only one name on it. The general title would be, "The verbal behavior of bilinguals in everyday speech."

Dounia was busy preparing other exams so at first I was the only one to do the required literature search which would help us write the first part. I obtained an entry card to the lovely Bibliothèque Nationale on the rue de Richelieu, and started reading books on bilingualism. There were far fewer back then, but some of them were already classics, such as Uriel Weinreich's *Languages in Contact*, and Einar Haugen's *The Norwegian Language in America: A Study in Bilingual Behavior*. I also discovered the work of the French Andrée Tabouret-Keller, the Canadian Wallace Lambert, and the American James P. Soffietti, among others.

The practical part of our work was made up of a questionnaire, a conversation *à trois* with each participant, and two small tests. Everything was done orally. In the questionnaire, we asked questions about our participants' biography, their linguistic behavior in their two languages, as well as questions relating to which languages they thought in, and the language(s) used in behaviors such as counting, praying, arguing, etc. In the conversation, we asked each bilingual to talk in the language that was addressed to him/her. I spoke English and Dounia, French, at different moments during the conversation. The topics covered everyday subjects such as politics, the European Common Market (now the European Union), literature, music, painting, fashion, etc. Finally, the tests were words and expressions, in either English or French, that they had to translate into the other language, as well as pictures that they had to describe in whichever language they chose to speak.

Looking back at this work after a whole career researching bilinguals, I can find so many things that could have been improved, but we had had no methodological guidance and did our best at the time. Having a thesis advisor in the French university system back then did not mean that he or she would spend time with you on your study, and give you advice on how to prepare it, run it, and analyze the data. You saw your advisor at the very beginning, maybe once or twice during the year, and then at the final exam. We tested 40 French–English bilinguals which we broke down into early and late bilinguals. Among the latter, we had two subgroups: English dominant and French dominant. We made sure not to use students only and had diplomats, business people, secretaries, stay-at-home parents, and so on.

The analysis of the data we obtained was the most basic possible (neither of us had any statistical knowledge at the time) and essentially was made up of tables with no summary statistics and not a hint of inferential statistics. We also wrote a paragraph or two on each bilingual summarizing his/her results. Our work was heavily influenced by the state of knowledge of bilingualism at that time. For example, few researchers made a clear distinction between interferences—deviations from the language being written or spoken stemming from the influence of the other, deactivated language—and mixed language behavior, such as code-switching and borrowing, due to the presence of other bilinguals. In our case, participants were in a bilingual environment because they knew we could speak both languages and so many mixed their languages. We recognized this by coining the expression "parler bilingue" (bilingual speech) but we still had a tendency to give more importance to interferences in our data analysis when, in fact, we might have been dealing with mixed speech. In the conclusion, we noted that all our participants were proud of being bilingual, although a few did mention their difficulty in adapting to their two cultures.

As I leaf through this thesis today, I realize how little I knew about the scientific aspects of bilingualism . . . and about language research methodology. This said, both Dounia and I enjoyed interacting with our participants, as they with us, and it is clear this first project opened up the way to my future research on the topic.

6
May 68 and Vincennes

J ust as my fourth year as a student at the Sorbonne was
drawing to a close, I lived through, and took part in, the
May 68 events in Paris. It was to be the start of an amazing
six years in my life as a doctoral student and a young academic.

May 68

In the afternoon of May 3, 1968, I was walking back to the
Quartier Latin from the language lab in Censier, a university
building near the Jardin des Plantes. It was a sunny day and I was
enjoying my walk through old parts of Paris: rue Mouffetard, rue
de l'Estrapade, and Place du Panthéon. As I arrived at Place de la
Sorbonne, right in front of the main university building, I saw
numerous blue police buses belonging to the CRS (Compagnies
Républicaines de Sécurité), part of the French police that deals
with crowd and riot control. They were in front of the Sorbonne
herding students into buses to take them to the Centre Beaujon,
situated on the other side of the Seine, where their identity cards
were checked and where they were occasionally beaten up. Just
then, I saw students coming down the Boulevard St. Michel,
chanting "Libérez nos camarades" (Release our comrades). They

A Journey in Languages and Cultures. First edition. François Grosjean.
© François Grosjean 2019. First published 2019 by Oxford University Press.

started throwing cobblestones at the CRS who responded with teargas grenades. And then things escalated into real violence. Thus started the May 68 events that I was to witness first-hand and also take part in.

There had been some unrest on the Nanterre university campus outside Paris for some weeks and when the buildings were closed, some students had decided to come into Paris and hold a meeting in the Sorbonne itself. They arrived on the morning of May 3, and everything went smoothly until the early afternoon when a rumor spread that a right-wing group was coming to attack them. Some students started finding objects to defend themselves with, and faced with the prospect of violence, the President of the university (the "recteur") stopped all classes. He then made the fatal mistake of calling in the police to evacuate the main courtyard and closing down the Sorbonne. There had been a long tradition that the police never entered university buildings but on that day, not only did they come in, but they also pushed the students into buses, many of whom were simply coming out of their courses. Had they simply let them go, the May events would probably not have got under way. Clashes between students on the boulevards and the CRS got worse that day, small barricades were constructed by the students, and the Quartier Latin was turned into what looked like a war zone.

I walked around the Quartier Latin the next day and saw the remnants of the very violent confrontation between the CRS and the students. The Sorbonne remained closed and was totally surrounded by police. The arrested students were slowly released from Beaujon but a handful were condemned to two months in prison. The student and teacher unions agreed on three popular demands: the freeing of all students, the reopening of the Sorbonne, and the removal of the police from the Quartier

Latin. There followed daily demonstrations which often ended, late at night, in more violence. I marched peacefully with hundreds of other students chanting our demands, but never took part in the violence that followed. One night, that of May 10, was particularly bad, with whole avenues crisscrossed with barricades which the police then attacked. I remember walking up the Boulevard St. Michel earlier that night and seeing the barricades being built and telling myself that the night was going to be very long...and very violent.

The government finally gave in after a week, and by the morning of May 13 the students still under arrest had been freed, the Sorbonne had been reopened, and the police had left the Quartier. I lived so close to the Sorbonne that as soon as I heard on the radio of the government's decision, I walked to the main building. I was one of the first to enter it and couldn't believe that everything was so quiet after more than a week of sirens wailing, grenades exploding, chants from demonstrations, and so on. Later that day, the Sorbonne was occupied by students, as were other university buildings. Then began several weeks of general assemblies, committee meetings, spontaneous discussion groups, and so on.

All topics were discussed, many political, but I spent most of my time in meetings proposing changes to the university which I knew well by then, having just finished my fourth year. The problems were many: overcrowded lecture halls and classes, little contact between the faculty and the students, antiquated academic programs, no student involvement in program changes, crumbling facilities, lack of financial support, few ties to the outside world, etc. Part of the problem was that a happy few could pursue their studies in the "grandes écoles," elite colleges that you entered after passing a competitive exam, whereas the majority were enrolled in the universities. The grandes écoles only took in a very small percentage of students but could count on about a third of the budget given to higher education, which was disproportionate. Graduates from the grandes écoles were assured of a prestigious job after their studies (they still are to this day) whereas graduates from the university had far more difficulties finding a job, many remaining unemployed for long periods of time.

My own institute, l'Institut d'anglais, right next to the Boulevard St. Michel, had been occupied and many of the group discussions leading to proposals for change took place there. The meetings were very orderly and people actually listened to each other, and built on what was said, something I was not used to that much in France. Every speaker was treated with respect and consideration. It was as if we all knew that the moment was exceptional and that we could maybe, just maybe, build together a better and fairer university. Basically, and without quite realizing it, we were applying one of the May 68 slogans, "Soyez réalistes, demandez l'impossible" (Be realistic, ask for the impossible).

When a general assembly was needed to accept what had been discussed, we would go to the Sorbonne and meet in the lecture halls there such as the "amphithéâtre Richelieu" or the "amphithéâtre Descartes." What was very special was that the younger faculty took part in these larger meetings, but also in the smaller ones, and it was the first time, for many of us, that we could actually speak to them outside of classes. The full professors, who were more conservative, stayed home with one or two exceptions, the most prominent being Antoine Culioli. He quickly stood out as THE faculty leader in our institute.

For several weeks, we lived in this other world where anything and everything seemed possible. Every day we would see creative posters printed overnight at the Ecole des Beaux Arts by the students there, as well as slogans tagged on walls, some of which are now famous: "Sous les pavés, la plage" (Under the cobblestones, the beach); "Il est interdit d'interdire" (It is forbidden to forbid); "Cours camarade, le vieux monde est derrière toi" (Run comrade, the old world is behind you!). When barricades blocked an avenue, or the police simply closed it down, we would walk in the middle of it, with the traffic lights still working. It was very eery, especially in the evenings.

The May events, which rapidly involved others segments of society (factory and transport workers, store personnel, members of the media, etc.), attracted hundreds of reporters from across the world. France was on general strike, and Paris, the city of lights, was literally on fire, at least in the Quartier Latin. The English-speaking media looked for students and faculty who could tell them what was happening, and they came to the Institut d'anglais. Because of my bilingualism, I was one of the students they interviewed, and Culioli represented the faculty. We would often find ourselves side by side, facing microphones and cameras, explaining why we were occupying the Sorbonne and the changes we wanted to bring.

One notable reporter who came to us was Olivier Todd, mentioned in the preceding chapter, who at that time worked for the BBC. I remember vividly that one day he was interviewing me and the camera was rolling. He asked me about the violence the night before and I replied that it had indeed taken place, in what I thought was a subdued British tone. He stopped the camera, told me to be a bit more emphatic and upset *à la française*, and then signaled to restart the camera. It was my first foray into the world of journalism and I understood then why several takes are sometimes necessary during interviews. But in this particular case, there was an added element. Both Todd and I were French–English biculturals and should have been on the same wave length. However, he was letting his French side react, and wanted a strong reaction, whereas I was thinking of those who would see me and was letting my English side speak. I was therefore more restrained. This said, it was one of the first times that I saw the positive side of being bilingual and bicultural. I could speak about what was going on in France in comprehensible terms for a British or American public, and I found this to be a very rewarding experience. A few weeks later I was told that people at Ratcliffe had recognized me, despite my beard, and one of them had cried out, "Hey, that's Frank Grosjean!"

By the middle of June, the Sorbonne and other buildings had been freed up but the reform movement continued in the following months in more sedate ways. Those events clearly had a major impact on who I was, and the teacher and researcher I was going to be. Even though I was sometimes criticized in my later years for my May 68 personality, I always tried to respect and listen to those I interacted with and worked with, I remained a firm believer in group discussion and, if at all possible, group decision, I strove to reduce the distance between the various hierarchical levels in the university, and I remained a reformer at heart.

I had been so taken up by the events that spring that I had problems going on vacation when the university closed over the summer. France went back to its regular life, with its habit of closing everything down in the second part of July and in August, and left many of us stranded. So I went off to the Pyrenees to take part in another work camp, building a milk pipeline for local farmers. When I came back in September, I was undecided on what to do. Should I prepare the *agrégation*, a competitive exam leading to a permanent position as a high school teacher, and maybe a position later at the university level, or should I continue and do a Ph.D. (a *doctorat*). I decided on the latter even though there were no guarantees I would find a position once I had finished, unlike in English-speaking countries at the time where that diploma was highly regarded.

Whilst I looked around for a thesis advisor, I took a part-time job teaching spoken English to business people in a language school near the rue de Rivoli. It was a fine experience as the groups were small and the students highly motivated to improve their English. We also put the emphasis on speech production and comprehension, two areas of language I was to study in the years to come.

Vincennes

At some point, I heard that an experimental university center was going to open a few months later, in January 1969, in the Bois de Vincennes, and that they were hiring at all levels. In response to the May events, the Education Minister, Edgar Faure, had agreed to have two such centers, the other—the Centre Dauphine—being dedicated to economics and management in the former NATO building on the other side of Paris. I applied for an assistant's position at the "Centre Universitaire Expérimental de Vincennes," in Anglo-American studies, and after a few weeks' wait, I obtained it. It's interesting to note that three faculty members involved in English studies, two at the Sorbonne, Pierre Dommergues and Bernard Cassen, and one at Nanterre, Hélène Cixous, had been instrumental in the conception and building of the Centre, and all that in a matter of months.

Vincennes as it was called—it is now the University of Paris 8—was an amazing place in its early years and a kind of dream come true for those who wanted a different, and more humane, university (I was to teach there for six years). It was open to regular students but also to people who did not have their *baccalauréat*. It also welcomed people who worked during the day and hence courses were offered until ten o'clock at night and on Saturdays. It accepted students from abroad, and developed exchange programs, such as with American universities, many years before programs such as Erasmus in Europe got under way. As for the studies themselves, topics not normally found in the Arts and Humanities, such as mathematics, computer sciences, psychoanalysis, etc., were offered along with other more traditional subjects. And students could combine these the way they wanted to in order to obtain a degree.

The year was broken down into semesters, something new at the time, the credit system was brought in, and programs included majors and minors. Large group lectures were often replaced by courses in small groups, and the faculty were encouraged to team up for special courses, and to interact with students. All this existed in American universities but was totally new in the antiquated French academic system. As for the faculty themselves, many prestigious professors were attracted to Vincennes including Michel Foucault, Gilles Deleuze, François Chatelet, and so on. And academics from abroad were invited in for permanent positions (e.g. Christine Brook-Rose, the British writer and critic) or visiting positions (e.g. Anthony Sampson, the author of *Anatomy of Britain*, among other books).

The newly hired faculty started work in January 1969 and discovered totally new buildings with armchairs in the corridors, offices that were well equipped, lecture halls with audio-visual material, language labs, recording studios, etc.—something we simply weren't used to normally. As an assistant, I was placed in the oral language teaching section, and became the coordinator for the teaching of oral comprehension. A colleague, Alain Deschamps, looked after oral production (pronunciation and structural exercises), along with others, and Margo Callahan, an American, was in charge of a team teaching spoken American English, something totally new at the time.

That first year was relatively hectic as we didn't have any teaching material and we basically had to build it from scratch. Since I was in charge of oral comprehension, I worked with native speakers such as Vivienne Méla or Kobi Lewin to prepare tapes and the answer sheets that went with them. I also recorded interviews with visiting academics (I remember taping Anthony Sampson with his deep voice and slow tempo) and included tapes with songs such as Leonard Cohen's *Suzanne*. I even bought a portable tape recorder which I took to England to record programs by the BBC (there was, of course, no internet at that time) which I then prepared for use in the classroom.

The first year had started late and so we finished in July, tired out but also happy we had made it through. One day, that summer, I saw a group of third year students in the corridor outside our office. I went up to them and they told me that they were organizing a party, and asked me if I could come. One of them, a tall and very lovely young lady whom I had noticed before because of the sombrero she sometimes wore, insisted that I come. I didn't promise anything as I had another party planned. That evening, as that first party was winding down, I suddenly remembered the students' party. It wasn't far from where I was and so I drove to it on my scooter. It was still in progress, and the young lady was there. We started talking, then dancing, and a few hours later, as dawn was breaking, I invited her to come and walk along the Seine in my *quartier*. She accepted … and we haven't left one another since then. Lysiane and I were married only three months later and we are now in our 50th year together. I cannot imagine how my life would have been had I not gone to that other party.

Harlan Lane

My doctoral research was on hold during that first year but it was to get an enormous boost in the second year. Our department had invited a young American professor of psychology, Harlan Lane, for at least one year. He had a position at the University of Michigan, after having studied at Columbia and Harvard, and despite his young age, 33, he was already quite famous. His article, *The motor theory of speech perception: A critical review*, had made a huge splash, among many other articles he had written. He had decided to take some time off in France, a country that was to become his second home, and was only too pleased to have a position both at Vincennes and at the Sorbonne, in the Laboratoire de phonétique.

The department head asked us what kind of graduate courses we would like and I proposed a course on speech perception and comprehension, a course on statistics, and a research seminar on second language comprehension. Harlan agreed and did a wonderful job giving us the basics in psycholinguistics and statistics, and organizing our research on speech comprehension. I was totally captivated by this young professor who was such an amazing teacher, a caring advisor, and so full of ideas for projects. I knew after only a few weeks that I had found my future area of expertise, psycholinguistics, and the thesis advisor I was looking for. Because he was a visiting professor, he could not take on doctoral students officially but he was prepared to advise me unofficially. So I went to see Antoine Culioli who accepted for me to work with Harlan even though he, Culioli, would be my official advisor.

We agreed that I would work on speech rate and its components (articulation rate, number and duration of pauses) and that there would be two parts to my thesis. One part on how it is that speech rate is perceived by the listener and the speaker, i.e. extraphonic and autophonic rate, and the other part on how rate and pauses play a role in speech comprehension by non-native speakers. Harlan helped me design the appropriate studies and guided me each step of the way. He also gave me access to a pen recorder (Mingograph) in the Laboratoire de phonétique to examine the distribution of speech and silence in continuous speech. For the data analysis, most notably analyses of variance, we even went together to buy a Friden electromechanical calculator on my scooter in the only store that had one in Paris. He then showed me how to use it.

I was simply amazed that a professor was prepared to spend so much time and energy guiding someone's research. I was to discover later that this was the American way of doing things and I enjoyed every minute of our time together. I suppose that for Harlan, not only was he doing what he had agreed to do, but it was a way for him to continue part of his research program while helping young and upcoming scientists learn the trade. Our partnership worked perfectly and out of those Paris years came a number of papers we published together in the prestigious *Journal of Experimental Psychology*.

Parallel to working with Harlan, I undertook some independent research with a colleague, Alain Deschamps, on temporal variables in English and French spontaneous speech. These variables include both global speech rate and articulation rate but also all the types of pauses we produce as speakers: silent and filled pauses, drawls, repetitions, and false starts. We compared 30 speakers in each language interviewed on radio, and obtained some very interesting findings such as that the global rate is the same in the two languages (no, French speakers do not talk faster). However, the distribution of silent pauses is different. Because of the grammatical structure of each language, there are fewer but longer pauses in French whereas in English, pauses are more numerous but shorter. We also uncovered that the total number of filled pauses and drawls, combined together, is identical in the two languages but that speakers of French produce almost as many drawls as filled pauses, whereas English speakers insert many more filled pauses than drawls.[1] This latter difference is due to the fact that there are more syllables that end with a vowel in French, and hence they can be lengthened into drawls.

While doing this research, both for my Ph.D. and with Alain Deschamps, I had read many papers by a British psycholinguist, Frieda Goldman-Eisler, who was a professor at University College, London. Since I was going back fairly frequently to England to make recordings for the oral comprehension course at Vincennes, I asked her if I could come and see her. Because of the very academic, very dry prose, used in her articles, I expected to find a rather strict and distant person. I was also still under the impression developed in France that professors were all rather aloof and rather cold. I was therefore taken by surprise to find a grandmother-type lady in her sixties, with a wonderful smile and kind manners, who offered me a cup of tea when I arrived. She also showed real interest in my work and was very supportive of it, giving me some very good advice. People like Harlan Lane and Frieda Goldman-Eisler, each in their own way, were showing me that research could be fascinating and exciting. I was definitely hooked... and still am some 50 years later!

I finished the practical work for my Ph.D. in sixteen months and wrote up my thesis in English. Lysiane then kindly translated it into French for me. This showed, yet again, how unsure I was about my written academic French which I no longer used much as I was teaching oral English. I then waited half a year before defending it with Antoine Culioli and Harlan Lane since there were various strikes slowing down the university. I was almost 26 when the defense finally took place.

On the family front, Lysiane and I moved to a small town just on the other side of the Paris city limits, Saint-Maur, very close to where her parents lived. They had made me part of their family and I could finally put those very lonely years in Paris behind me, although moments of solitude still haunt me to this day. It is there that we welcomed our first born, Cyril. I immediately became attached to this gorgeous little baby and set about giving him the care and love I would have enjoyed when I was his age. Those first months with baby Cyril are engraved in my memory as a time of pure bliss. But it was also a time of hard work as I continued my university job whilst working on various research projects, some with Harlan Lane. Lysiane, who also taught English, would work during the day and I would take the late afternoon and evening slots so that Cyril had a caretaker with him at all times. Those few years in Saint-Maur with baby Cyril were the start of our young family life.

After several years in France, much to my regret, Harlan Lane finally went back to the United States to occupy a position at the University of California in San Diego. In just a few years, he had introduced me to the field that was to be mine for the rest of my career, had been a role model in how to teach and do research, and had launched me as a researcher in speech and language processing. Just before saying goodbye, I told him that if ever he saw a way of getting me over to the United States, Lysiane and I would be willing to move over there for a year or two.

In the early part of 1974, when I was in my sixth year at Vincennes, Harlan wrote that he was to become the Chairperson of the Psychology Department at Northeastern University in Boston. Would I like to come over to help him set up a psycho-linguistics research laboratory which would study, among other things, the sign language of the deaf? Whilst in San Diego, he had discovered American Sign Language and had undertaken some experimental work with Ursula Bellugi and Penny Boyes Braem. After talking to Lysiane about it, I jumped at the opportunity. Things were slowly unwinding at Vincennes; this was due to the constant attacks from the Ministry of Education which no longer supported this "left wing" university, and which refused to give it the funds needed for an ever increasing student population. In addition, various extreme left-wing groups were making life difficult for the faculty who wanted to teach and for the students who wanted to learn. Strikes were frequent and the furniture and teaching material were not well maintained or were actually disappearing. Vincennes was simply no longer the "dream university" we had had for a few years at its beginning. So I told Harlan that I would be thrilled to come over for a year and that Vincennes was willing to give me a leave of absence for that period of time. I set about obtaining a Fulbright-Hays grant which came through in a few months. Not once did I think that I would never return to the university where I had started my career.

A new life in the United States

In early July 1974, the three of us, Lysiane, baby Cyril and I, drove up to Belgium and took the daily Sabena flight from Brussels to New York. When we got to the terminal, we were told that Cyril also needed a visa, even if it was stamped on one of our passports (he didn't have his own) and so we had to wait for the American Consulate to open the next day. The flight was long, the longest we had ever flown, and even more so as Cyril couldn't stay in his seat—he was only 22 months old—and we had to chase him all over the plane.

Our first year

What struck us first when we arrived at John F. Kennedy Airport, where we were to take another plane to Boston, was how big everything was: huge cars and trucks and buses, big TV screens, large terminals . . . and also how hot it was. We had hit that time of the year when the East Coast swelters in its heat and humidity. After a three hour wait, which seemed much longer with a tired-out toddler who hadn't slept in hours, we finally arrived in Boston where a couple, Michael and Jiuan Terman, kindly greeted us and took us to their home in Cambridge. And there, the first impression was how cool, almost too cool, the air conditioning was in that hot and humid weather.

Other impressions marked us the next few days and are still vivid in our minds: the distance to walk from one place to another when you don't have a car, the very bumpy sidewalks and sometimes no sidewalks at all, the proximity of different neighborhoods, from the very well-to-do to the poor, the trash in some streets that Cyril wanted to play with…and still that heat and humidity, and the contrast between the outside and the air-conditioned stores and houses. We started looking for an apartment and went from one part of the city to the other, lowering our expectations as we found that the rents were high, and the combination of my future salary with my grant was much lower than what I had earned in France.

We finally found a one-bedroom apartment in Central Square, Cambridge, just behind the City Hall, and started looking for a mattress, a table, and some chairs. We thought, "We have all that back in France, in storage," but then came back to our new reality—we were thousands of miles away from home and in a totally new country. Our next search was for a second-hand car as everyone told us we couldn't do without one and that public transport simply wasn't good enough, at least in those days. We found a nine-year-old Ford station wagon which for us was absolutely huge when compared to the Citroen 2 CV we had had in France. Unfortunately, it wasn't in good shape and the radiator had to be replaced almost at once (we couldn't do more than five miles before it overheated). Then the whole motor had to be replaced and we realized that we had bought a lemon.

Lysiane started looking for a part-time daycare for Cyril as she wanted to continue working on her Ph.D. during the day, and she came back one day to tell me that she had found one: the Oxford

Street Daycare Cooperative. She had visited it that afternoon and described how all the kids were outside in the parking lot when she arrived, splashing around naked in the large puddles following a sudden rain storm. It was a co-op daycare and parents were involved in running it and took turns cleaning it at the weekends. Interacting with other parents helped us settle in and reduced just a bit the culture shock we felt that first summer.

I started work at Northeastern only a few days after arriving as I was in charge of undergraduate statistics that summer semester. It was taught using the PSI method (Personalized System of Instruction) where students studied modules, did exercises, and came to a central location (it was called Psych Central) to get help if they needed it. They then took a test and if they passed it, they could move on to the next module. For a subject like statistics, this was a very interesting approach but it was also used for more traditional topics, such as Psychology 101, and there the students weren't as pleased with the method. Part of my job was to recruit and interact with the TA's (undergraduate and graduate teaching assistants) who tutored the students and gave them their tests. My own knowledge of statistics was not what it is today and I really had to play catch-up for the first few months—just one of a set of challenges I had to meet that first year.

On the research front, I was given an office that I shared with another colleague, right next to Harlan's laboratory. When I arrived, the lab was totally empty except for a new Digital PDP 11 computer which no one knew how to use. Harlan and I quickly went on a crash course at DEC (Digital Equipment Company) in Maynard and then with the help of a young research assistant from Electrical Engineering, we started working with it. I learned to program in Basic and very quickly I had a set of computer programs ready to allow us to do simple descriptive and inferential statistics. We slowly equipped the lab, bought audio equipment as well as some video recorders for our sign language projects, and even hired a deaf research assistant (I'll talk about this in the next chapter).

That summer went by very quickly but we stayed in Cambridge/ Boston as I had to work and our car was simply not reliable enough for trips in the country. One weekend, Harlan lent us his second car, a Chevy Vega, and we finally discovered the surrounding countryside. We fell under the charm of places like Concord and Lexington and discovered Walden Pond which was to become "our" lake to swim in during the summer, walk on when it was iced up in winter, and walk around in all seasons. We then discovered the little towns north of Boston such as Marblehead, Manchester and its beach, Rockport, etc. and realized that we were in a very lovely part of New England.

Our first friends were graduate students at Northeastern as we were very close in age to them and I was a sort of postdoc even though I had been given the title of Visiting Assistant Professor. They invited us to their parties and even on hikes in New Hampshire. We quickly knew the topics that we could discuss and the ones that were less popular such as politics, a major subject of discussion among friends in France but less so in the States after the Vietnam War. Another topic to be avoided was comparing countries, with their advantages and disadvantages. On one occasion, I made some kind of comparison between France and America to a teaching assistant who replied that if I didn't like it in the US, I should return to France. I was taken aback as this was purely an intellectual comparison and I put this on my list of topics to keep away from.

Of course, the shock we had felt on arriving remained for a while and there were so many things to talk about with Lysiane every day, something I had not been able to do with anyone when I had moved from England to France ten years before. Some things were more serious, some a bit less. For example, the space one had to leave while standing in line was much greater than in France, and I noticed that if I used the French distance, the person ahead of me showed some discomfort. Even the French clothes we wore could be a problem. I had rather short shorts whereas American men wore long, baggy shorts at that time. One day, a TA told me, "Wow, those are really short shorts, François!" I took this as a clear signal that I should be careful with the way I dressed. But at other times, we were thrilled by what we found. For example, Cyril was an inquisitive and very lively toddler whom some French adults didn't take easily to. But in the States, he had a lot of success. One day at Walden Pond, he wandered off to see a police officer a bit further away, and came back wearing his cap and holding his whistle. This would have been totally impossible in France back then.

By the time we went back home for Christmas, six months later, we had clearly started the process of adjusting to our new culture. We realized that deep down the life we had led in France before coming over, the way we had worked at Vincennes, and the relationship we had developed with people after May 68, were not fundamentally different from what we had found in the States. We were happy to tell our friends how we were settling in, but we found that some of their reactions were rather cold. They were critical of our decision to go to the States, and some bashed the country we had chosen to move to in front of us. Even on such banal topics as the use of computers, they were disdainful that one could use them to do one's research. We were basically living what many others had lived before us. As I wrote in my book, *Bilingual: Life and Reality*, the stages that take place in migration, at least to the United States, are now well studied—arrival, isolation, culture shock, and more or less rapid acculturation. The literature mentions the migrants' idealization of their home country, the return shock they experience when they see that "back home" no longer matches their dreams and memories, and the more or less permanent acceptance of a migratory status.[1] We returned to Cambridge with the aim of settling in and enjoying our stay in the US.

Our first winter in New England was also a bit of a shock. It was very cold and we were simply not well equipped to face it with our European clothes, so we went to Sears to get what we needed; we found many winter clothes for Cyril in thrift stores. The snowstorms were also a surprise with their large amounts of snow in a very short time, and then the clear blue sky that appeared afterwards.

Cyril quickly got used to his daycare and started to become the little American in our family. He would watch Mr. Rogers' Neighborhood, Sesame Street, and Captain Kangaroo on television, and would repeat all kinds of expressions he heard. Without us realizing it, our little French boy was becoming bilingual, and was using more and more English with us. At first we would only speak to him in French and try to get him to answer back in that language, but enforcing French became difficult. With time, he used less French with us especially in front of other children. I personally recall the day he told me outside, "Dad, speak like all the other dads," by which he meant something like, "Since you also speak English, and English is the language used here, and I don't want to be different from the others, then let's speak English together instead of French." Cyril became a dormant bilingual and we sometimes wondered how much French he continued to understand. What was happening to him is well reported in the bilingualism literature but we were experiencing it first-hand. We didn't worry too much as we thought we wouldn't be staying that long in the States and his French would be reactivated in no time once we got back.

We stay on

At work, Harlan and I wrote grant proposals for our research on speech and sign and obtained them, much to our delight. At the end of the first year, Lysiane and I decided to stay a second year since my J1 visa was valid for two years. My summer salary was now covered by our grants and I could therefore concentrate on research and do a bit less teaching. I continued my work on temporal variables (rate, pausing) and compared how they behave in spoken languages (English and French) and in sign languages (American Sign Language).

At the start of our second year, we took a trip up to Quebec and something very special occurred as we were nearing the border. I switched on the radio and we suddenly heard the French singer, Mireille Mathieu, interpreting one of her well-known songs. All our pent-up needs for things French in our daily American life suddenly rose to the surface and for the next hour we dreamed of finding France on the other side of the border. We didn't, of course, and it took us a bit of time to accept that Quebec was a specific entity in North America with its own French dialect and its own culture. During that trip, we toured Gaspésie and one day we stopped at a "salle à manger" (restaurant) to have lunch. The waitress came up to us and offered us two kinds of soups. We understood the first one but not the second ("soupe à l'alphabet," alphabet soup). We asked her to repeat it, and say it a third time, before asking for "la première" (the first soup mentioned). We later told ourselves that she must have felt we were behaving like French purists. On another occasion, we stopped off for gas and I made the mistake of speaking to the gas attendant in French. He understood what I said perfectly but I simply didn't comprehend his reply. I found a way of answering more or less correctly and saved the situation.

During our second year in the United States, we realized that we were hooked and we agreed to stay even longer. A one-year visit was transforming itself into a migration, although we didn't quite realize it at the time. Many of the things that related to how people lived and worked, what they ate, how they socialized and so on, were starting to be quite familiar, but there were still some hidden customs that we had to be introduced to, most notably Thanksgiving. When our first Thanksgiving weekend had arrived in our first year, we had thought it was like any other extended weekend. On the Thursday itself (we didn't yet know it was called Thanksgiving Day), we had simply gone on a hike in the nearby hills. As we were coming back in the afternoon, we had found everything terribly quiet in our neighborhood, and we had no inkling of what was going on in millions of homes all over the country.

In the fall of our second year, quite by chance, we met an American friend, Myrna Norris, whom we had known a few years before at Vincennes. We started chatting with her and at some point she asked us if we would like to celebrate Thanksgiving with her family. We accepted, not quite realizing what that meant. We were asked to arrive at 2 p.m. which we thought was a bit late for lunch (we had little knowledge of how the day was organized) and we were greeted warmly by her parents, siblings, cousins, friends, and many children. Then, as we went from the kitchen to the children's room, and then to the living room where a football game was showing on TV, we realized that we wouldn't be eating for some time yet. That afternoon and then evening, we discovered a totally new celebration with its well-established traditions, both culinary and social.

A year later, our first Thanksgiving Day initiation long over, we weren't really thinking about doing anything special. It is well known though that migrant parents acculturate to a new culture in part through their children, and Cyril started talking about it as well as the size of the turkey we would have and all the trimmings that would go with it. So we decided to give the meal a try. In addition, since the playground we took him to was next to a football field, we watched with interest the local game that morning without really understanding the rules. Little by little, Thanksgiving became part of our family tradition, just like Halloween. Our son, through his contacts at school and his neighborhood friends, knew more about these holidays than we did and was instrumental in helping us get things straight.

With time we felt sufficiently comfortable with the Thanksgiving menu that we invited a Belgian couple, Didier and Suzanne, who had just arrived to join us on that day. It was fun telling them about the tradition (we had done our homework beforehand) and to talk about the events that take place. I had started enjoying American football and had learned from friendly colleagues, Carlos and Steve, what to look at, and not look at, when watching a game, so we switched on the TV. Eventually our Belgian friends took over organizing the Thanksgiving dinner and, over the years, the number of faces around the table increased as our children were born (their four and our additional one). We then continued this tradition of going to their house on that day.

Cyril was definitely an important conduit to things American. It started with little things such as dressing up like the other kids for Halloween and going trick or treating. Then he would invite other children to sleep over at our place. And then he got into sports and wanted to play hockey. So we enrolled him in a program, found him all the right equipment, and like other hockey parents, took him to his training and his games. He then wanted to play baseball and so we got him to join a little league baseball team. We would take him to his practices and we learned about the sport through him. After a few years, he moved on to others sports, and was no longer interested in baseball. But I was, and he left me stranded watching baseball games by myself.

Since I had always kept open the option of returning to Vincennes, which by then had become the University of Paris 8, I asked Antoine Culioli in 1978 if I could defend my *doctorat d'Etat*, an habilitation thesis that still existed at that time and that allowed one to become a full professor. He accepted for me to present sixteen publications preceded by a cover chapter that introduced and integrated them. Friends in Paris—Bernadette Grancolas, Michèle Mittner, and Jean-Yves Dommergues— helped me prepare the physical copies of the thesis, and when everything was set, I went over to defend it in front of a jury of four professors. All went well and I became a "docteur d'Etat" at the age of 32, one of the youngest I believe in the field of linguistics. That very same year, just after the Blizzard of 78, we welcomed little Pierre into our family.

A new program, teaching and research

The Psychology Department at Northeastern started the process of getting me a work permit and then applying for a longer-term visa. To make a case for keeping me and giving me tenure, we agreed that I would help start and head a major and minor in linguistics. This was a huge challenge as the project had to be accepted at all levels—department, college, and university. Since courses in linguistics already existed in five different departments—Psychology, English, Modern Languages, Philosophy and Religion, and Sociology/Anthropology—we decided to make the program interdisciplinary. It was a success and after a few years, 21 of 22 students majoring in linguistics had graduated with honors.

On the teaching front, in addition to continuing statistics, I started offering courses and seminars in psycholinguistics. Many of them were interpreted in real time into American Sign Language for deaf students in the class. It is really at Northeastern that I realized how much I enjoyed teaching. My instructor and course grades were excellent and clearly the students liked the way I went about it. This led to my being a recipient of the Excellence in Teaching Award the first year it was proposed by the university. I have had time to reflect on why I was blessed with this ability and have found a number of reasons. First, I have always been passionate about what I teach, even with topics as dry as statistics or acoustic phonetics. Then, it is important that the course is well organized and well structured. It also needs to be taught at the right rhythm, neither too slowly nor too fast.

You also need to care about the students you have. You have to be aware of what they know about the topic at the beginning of the course and where you want to take them to by the end. This allows you to accompany them at just the right level, neither too easy nor too hard. Adding a bit of humor from time to time helps a lot. Being attuned to students' reactions is also crucial, as it allows you to explain a point once again, go faster on a particular topic, or slow down. Remaining polite and courteous is also very important, as is never censuring a student, either in public or in private. Students are doing you the privilege of coming to listen to you and you must show them respect. This said, teaching has always been a personal challenge and I can now admit that before each course I have the butterflies, and am sometimes fearful. And once a course is over, I invariably ask myself whether I have been clear and have explained things the right way. Only students' evaluations and exam results reassure me in the end.

On the research front, I slowly veered towards the on-line processing of language, most notably word recognition. I was greatly influenced in this by the pioneering work of William Marslen-Wilson and Lorraine Tyler whom I had met in the United States when they were still there. In order to prepare the stimuli for experiments, I asked Ken Stevens, professor at MIT, whether I could come to his lab to use the speech editing programs that Dennis Klatt has implemented on a PDP 12. He kindly accepted and I became a Research Affiliate in his department. The computer was in high demand and so I used it in the early hours of the morning, between 5.00 and 7.00 am, when I was sure I could have access to it. It is there that I saw that it was easy to cut up and present words in gates (segments) of increasing duration, from their beginnings to their ends. Thus, the very first gate might be the first 30 msec of the word, the second 60 msec, the third 90 msec, until the whole word had been presented. These gates could be presented in isolation or preceded by a verbal context. The participants in an experiment had to listen to the segment, write down the word they thought was being presented, and give a confidence rating.

With the data obtained from this gating task, the experimenter could work out the isolation point of a word (the size of the segment needed to identify the word), the confidence ratings at the isolation point and at the end of the word, and the word candidates proposed at each segment before the stimulus has been isolated. Even though I was to find out later that simpler versions of gating had been used by others, this was the first time that the full-fledged task was developed and used. The very first speech study I did using the gating paradigm[2] showed a context effect (words in context are recognized sooner than words out of context), a frequency effect (frequent words are recognized sooner than infrequent words), and a length effect (long words are recognized later than short words). It also allowed me look at the possibilities proposed before a word is recognized and the types of errors (garden paths) listeners can make whilst processing the word.

As I was developing the gating paradigm, and as soon as I saw the results I was obtaining, I knew that I was on to something important. All the more so when the study was written up and preprint versions had been sent to colleagues such as David Pisoni, the well-known speech perception specialist, who was enthusiastic about it. The paper was accepted without changes by *Perception and Psychophysics*. I was also able to show in a later paper that during the continuous processing of speech, not all words are recognized before their end.[3] This causes problems for models of word recognition that defend a totally sequential, left-to-right, word-by-word process.

Gating was off to having a long life in psycholinguistic research, not only with adult participants but also with children, without or with disorders, the elderly, aphasic patients, bilinguals (I will speak about this a bit later), as well as deaf persons using sign language. As for the phenomena that can be studied with it, there are many possibilities other than regular word recognition. Among these, we find the role of word stress, word morphology, and gender marking. It can even be used to study the prediction that takes place when one is listening to someone else speaking. I showed this at the level of prosody (intonation, stress, etc.) in a study where listeners heard segments of sentences that continued for 0, 3, 6, or 9 more words. They had to choose among the four possible endings which they never heard but which were presented to them in writing. Basing themselves on the prosody of the first part of the sentence only, the participants were surprisingly good at telling whether a sentence was over or not, and if it continued, whether it did so just a bit (3 more words) or a bit more (6 and 9 more words).[4]

I had been at Northeastern for at least six years when I met a theoretical linguist from Hampshire College, James (Jim) Gee, who was on leave in our department. We got on extremely well and became good friends. I greatly appreciated his kindness and his humor, and admired his knowledge of linguistics. Together we wrote a number of papers on sentence and discourse structure as well as on word recognition. For example, using two lines of research, one from linguistics and one from psycholinguistics, we accounted for performance structures of sentences (i.e. the structures based on experimental data as reported on previously[5]). We developed an algorithm based on the prosodic structures of sentences which was later used, to our surprise, by those developing the synthesis of continuous speech.[6] Jim was later to become a highly reputed specialist of new literacies and learning principles in video games.

Seven years after having arrived in the United States, I was awarded tenure and was promoted to Associate Professor. My family and I were basically set to stay permanently as there were very few positions available in France and there were so many things we enjoyed in our new country. I had also come to accept my Anglo-Saxon side fully and felt at ease with it. In addition, the children were basically American and didn't speak French. But there were also so many things we missed in Europe and so we kept all options open, as do many migrants who in the end may never make it back to their first countries.

8
Discovering sign language

When I had first arrived at Northeastern, and for a number of years thereafter, I worked on American Sign Language (ASL), a visual gestural language that mesmerized me. All language scientists have a wow moment in their profession and mine was when I was introduced to sign language and to the world of the deaf. I was simply overwhelmed by the beauty of this visual gestural language, by the history of deaf people, and by their different form of bilingualism, ASL and English.

This took place at the very start of the renaissance of sign language after a long period of rejection by educators of the deaf, and I am proud to have been a member of a research team, among others, that helped its rebirth. Few people know that American Sign Language had flourished in American schools for the deaf during the better part of the 19th century. Thomas Gallaudet, a deaf educator, had gone to Europe to learn how deaf children were educated, and he came back with Laurent Clerc, a deaf teacher who used sign language to teach deaf children. Clerc helped Gallaudet found the first school for the deaf in America, in Hartford, Connecticut. Sign language was used throughout the century until 1880 when an International Congress on the Education of the Deaf declared that it should no longer be used in

A Journey in Languages and Cultures. First edition. François Grosjean.
© François Grosjean 2019. First published 2019 by Oxford University Press.

schools for the deaf and that it should be replaced by speech. There followed practically a hundred years of "oralism" during which sign language was banned in schools and deaf children who used it were reprimanded and even punished.

By the early 1970s, thanks to the work of researchers like William Stokoe of Gallaudet College, a renaissance of sign language was taking place in the United States. Ursula Bellugi and Edward Klima at the Salk Institute in San Diego were among the academics who started studying sign language and who got others interested in it. Harlan Lane was one of those and when he left San Diego for Northeastern in 1974, he decided to dedicate part of his research to the psycholinguistics of sign language. I was thrilled to discover this totally different language and to collaborate with him on how it was perceived and produced.

Sign language research

Our first task was to hire a research assistant and we chose Marie Philip, a deaf native signer from a deaf family who had just finished her studies at Gallaudet. A year later she was joined by Ella Mae Lentz, another member of the deaf community. Both of them were to become extremely well known for their work in and around deafness. We hearing academics also had to learn sign language, and we took lessons with Marie and later with Barrie Schwartz, a sign language interpreter and teacher who had grown up in a deaf family. Another person who helped us get started was Ann Macintyre, also the hearing daughter of deaf parents, who was known in Boston for her sign interpretation of the news on television early in the morning, a first at the time.

The research Harlan and I undertook, along with a postdoc, Robin Battison, and a few research assistants, was aimed at a better understanding of how a manual visual language like ASL was produced by the hands, arms, face, and body, and how it was perceived visually. What aspects were specific to the modality, we asked, and what aspects were common to all languages, whatever their modality of production and perception. For example, in a 1979 study,[1] I showed that signers modify their global physical production rate by altering the time they spend articulating, whereas speakers do so by changing the time they spend pausing silently. When signers increase or decrease their pause time, however little they do so, they alter the number and the length of the pauses equally, whereas speakers of English primarily alter the number of silent pauses and leave their pause durations relatively constant, mainly for breathing reasons. I also found that signers retain their regular "quiet breathing" respiratory pattern across signing rates and inhale at locations independent of syntactic importance. In this they are quite unlike speakers who breathe at syntactic breaks.

I also published a few papers on the recognition of signs, using a visual gating approach.[2] I found, for example, that out of context only 51% of a sign is needed on average to be "isolated" (i.e. proposed for the first time when segments of increasing duration are proposed) whereas 83% of a spoken word is needed. This difference can probably be explained by the more simultaneous nature of the production of sublexical sign components whereas in speech, sounds and syllables occur sequentially. I continued this kind of research for some eight years.

Helping our French colleagues

Harlan Lane and I attended the World Congress of the World Federation of the Deaf in Washington, D.C. in early August, 1975, and met several members of the French delegation whom we then invited up to Boston. They told us that things were very difficult in France and that oralism was still rampant. In addition, there was no research taking place on sign language and American research papers were in English, a language very few of them knew. So we came up with the idea of dedicating a whole issue of the prestigious French academic journal *Langages* to sign language. We wrote to the editor who gave us his go-ahead. We then called on fellow researchers to write papers for the issue: Harry Markowicz on sign language myths and reality, Ronnie Wilbur on the linguistic description of sign language, Howard Poizner and Robin Battison on cerebral asymmetry for sign language, and James Woodward on some sociolinguistics aspects of French and American Sign Languages. Harlan concentrated on the history of sign language oppression in both France and the United States, and I wrote a paper on the psycholinguistics of sign language. With the exception of the latter, already in French, all the papers were translated from English into French—Lysiane was one of the translators—and the issue came out in 1979.[3]

When we saw the cover with "La langue des signes" in large characters below the title of the journal, we felt happy that we had contributed just a bit to the renaissance of sign language in France. It was only normal, after all, that America should give back something to France after Laurent Clerc's contribution to American Sign Language at the beginning of the preceding century. After the issue, followed a year later by a book in English with the same content,[4] we continued to tell French readers about our research through *Coup d'œil*, a small journal dedicated to deafness and sign language that Bernard Mottez and Harry Markowicz had started in Paris.

The bilingualism of the deaf

A few years later, whilst I was still at Northeastern, I started thinking and writing about bilingualism in the deaf community, in countries such as the United States or those in Western Europe. It is a form of minority language bilingualism in which the members of the community acquire and use both the minority language (the sign language used in the country) and the majority language (such as English in the US), in its written form and sometimes in its spoken or even signed form.[5] Deaf bilinguals show many similarities with hearing bilinguals: they are very diverse, many do not judge themselves to be bilingual, they use their languages for different purposes, in different domains of life, with different people, and they too navigate along a language continuum, restricting themselves to just one language in some situations, and mixing their languages in others.

But there are also differences with hearing bilinguals. First, there has been little recognition of deaf people's bimodal bilingual status. They are still seen by many as monolingual in the majority language whereas in fact many are bilingual in that language and in sign. Second, deaf bilinguals, because of their hearing loss, will usually remain bilingual throughout their lives and, for some, from generation to generation. A third difference, again due to hearing loss, is that the use of speech, and other majority language skills, may never be fully acquired by some deaf people. A fourth difference is that deaf bilinguals rarely find themselves in a monolingual signing situation since the majority of deaf people also know some English. Finally, the patterns of language knowledge and use appear to be somewhat different, and probably more complex, than in spoken language bilingualism. A sign language bilingual may use sign language with one interlocutor, a form of signed spoken language with another, a mixture of the two with a third, a form of simultaneous communication (sign and speech) with a fourth, and so on.

I also argued that many deaf people are bicultural: they live in two or more cultures (their family, friends, colleagues, etc. are either members of the deaf community or of the hearing world); they adapt, at least in part, to these cultures; and they blend aspects of them. Such factors as deafness in the family, age of onset of deafness, degree of hearing loss, type of education, etc. may lead some deaf people to have fewer contacts with the hearing world while others have more; thus their bicultural dominance can differ. There are at least two differences between the biculturalism of deaf people and that of the hearing. First, many people born deaf or deafened early in childhood still acculturate into the deaf culture—which will often become their dominant culture—relatively late (in adolescence, even adulthood). Their first years are mainly spent in the hearing world (90% of deaf people have hearing parents). In the case of the hearing, acculturation usually takes place early into the bicultural's dominant culture and then into the second culture. A second difference relates to dominance. Most deaf biculturals are usually dominant in one culture, the deaf culture, whereas hearing biculturals vary as to their dominance (Culture A, or Culture B, or a balance between the two cultures).

Deaf children and their right to be bilingual

In the world today, there is still no widespread acceptance that deaf children should be able to become bilingual. Very few are given the chance of mastering both a sign language and an oral language—in its spoken and/or written modality—from their earliest years on. A purely oral language education is preferred even though many may not adequately master it in the long run. I will always remember the example I saw during the World Congress of the Deaf in Washington, D.C. in 1975. A young French deaf adult had been robbed and had real problems explaining what had happened to him. He had been brought up solely with the oral method (speech and lip reading) and had not gotten very far with it. In reality, he could not speak or write. And, of course, he didn't know how to sign as sign language had been forbidden in schools for the deaf. So he was without a language and could only mime what had happened to him.

Research has shown the many advantages of allowing deaf children to know and use both a sign language and an oral language. It is the optimal combination that will allow these children to meet their many needs, that is, communicate early with their parents (first in sign and then, with time, maybe also in the oral language), develop their cognitive abilities, acquire knowledge of the world, communicate fully with the surrounding world, and acculturate into their two worlds. I have argued repeatedly that depending on the child, the two languages will play different roles in those allowed to become bilingual: some children will be dominant in sign language, others will be dominant in the oral language, and some will be balanced in their two languages.

It is still quite common for some professionals involved with deafness (doctors, speech-language pathologists, teachers, etc.) as well as for some parents to believe that the knowledge of sign language will hinder the development of the oral language in deaf children. The reasons for this belief are of three kinds. First, we still find the outdated view that bilingualism is the near-perfect mastery of two or more languages, that it is rare, and that it has negative consequences on the linguistic and cognitive development of children. Second, there are still numerous misunderstandings concerning sign language. Some still maintain that it is not a real language, that it will hinder the development of the spoken language of deaf children, and that those who defend sign language are automatically opposed to spoken language. All this is false. Third, there are realities that are not accepted by many professionals in deafness, and most notably members of the medical world. These realities are as follows: most deaf people belong to two worlds, the hearing world and the world of the deaf; a strictly auditory/oral education is no guarantee that deaf children will develop their spoken language sufficiently for unhindered communication with the outside world; and counting solely on technological progress (e.g. cochlear implants) and oral monolingualism is gambling on the development of the deaf child.

It is now well accepted that a first language that has been acquired normally, be it spoken or signed, will greatly enhance the acquisition and use of a second language. In the case of deaf children, whether they have a cochlear implant or not, sign language can be used early on to communicate while the oral language is being acquired; it can be used to express emotions, to explain things as well as to communicate about the other language; and linguistic skills acquired in sign such as discourse rules and even general writing skills, acquired through sign writing, can be transferred to the oral language. It has been shown that the better the children's skills are in sign language, the better they will know the oral language.

As for the oral language, it is usually the language of the child's parents, brothers and sisters, extended family, future friends, employers, etc. It is also this language, in its written modality mainly, that will be an important medium for the acquisition of knowledge. In addition, the deaf child's academic success and his/her future professional achievements will depend in large part on a good mastery of it, in its written and, if possible, spoken modality.

It is also important that deaf children and adolescents be given every opportunity to learn about the cultures they belong to, that they be able to interact with these cultures, and that they be able to go through the process of choosing the culture, or preferably, the cultures, they wish to identify with. Counting solely on the hearing culture and on an auditory/oral approach to language, because of recent technological advances, is betting on the deaf children's futures. It is putting at risk their cognitive, linguistic, and personal development and it is negating their need to acculturate into the two worlds that they belong to.

Many of the points made above are summarized in a short text that I was asked to write for a conference in Switzerland in the late 1990s, "The right of the deaf child to grow up bilingual." I first wrote it in French and then translated it into English. It appeared in many different publications and on the web, and since there was an increasing demand for it in other languages, I joined up with Carol Erting, professor at Gallaudet University and currently Provost there, to organize for its translation. Thanks to collaborators of the Signs of Literacy Program, the text is now available in 30 different languages which can be obtained freely on the web.[6] It is worth citing its two last lines, "One never regrets knowing several languages but one can certainly regret not knowing enough, especially if one's own development is at stake. The deaf child should have the right to grow up bilingual and it is our responsibility to help him/her do so."

Although with time I have personally lost most of the sign language[7] I learned as a young faculty at Northeastern due to lack of use, I have remained a defender of sign language, of its research, and of the bilingualism of deaf people, in particular of deaf children. I have continued to give interviews on this topic, the latest being in 2016.[8]

9

Life with Two Languages

I n 1979, I offered for the very first time a course on bilingualism. Different people attended it—not just students—such as Barrie Schwartz, one of our sign language interpreters, who wanted to learn about her own English–Sign Language bilingualism. Another person was an older graduate student, Carlos Soares, who was my age. Carlos had arrived in the United States at the age of 15 and had acquired English rapidly to the point of speaking it without an accent. He had always been interested in bilingualism and he asked me to be his Ph.D. advisor. I agreed and for the next three years, we formed a great team as I considered him more like a colleague than a student. His thesis was mainly concerned with language lateralization in bilinguals and monolinguals and we published several papers together.

I had not found a good introductory book to the field when I started preparing my course and so I looked into writing one myself based on all the notes I had. I asked Harlan Lane how I should go about it and whether he had a publisher to suggest. He had just published his *The Wild Boy of Aveyron* with Harvard University Press and he suggested that I approach his editor there, Eric Wanner. I did so rather naively and, much to my surprise, he showed interest in my project and asked me to show

A Journey in Languages and Cultures. First edition. François Grosjean.
© François Grosjean 2019. First published 2019 by Oxford University Press.

him a chapter. So I prepared the first chapter for him, "Bilingualism in the world," and after having it reviewed, he gave me a contract. I was only 34 years old, I had never written a book, and I had just been taken on by a prestigious university publisher; I could hardly believe it!

Einar Haugen

As all of this was taking place, I contacted a researcher on bilingualism I had so admired when working on my Master's thesis in Paris: Einar Haugen. I had re-read his books and articles, mainly on Norwegian–American bilinguals, and found out that he had retired from Harvard a few years before. So I wrote to him to see if I could meet him, and in his reply, he gave me his home phone number so that I could call him. I did so and asked him whether I should come to his office at Harvard; he agreed that we meet, but offered to do it at his home in Belmont, only a few miles from where I myself lived. We agreed on a time, 5 p.m. on a particular day, and he gave me indications on how to get there.

I was greeted by a rather tall, very genteel, elderly man who showed me into his living room. As he was getting me a drink, Eva Haugen came in and introduced herself. She looked like a dream grandmother with very fine features, her grey hair in a bun, a soft voice, and a wonderful smile. The first part of our meeting was more academic—I told Einar Haugen about my future book and we talked about topics in bilingualism such as language planning, language choice, code-switching, and so on. After about an hour, Eva joined us. Little by little, I realized that she too had had an impressive career as an author, editor, and translator of several books related to Norwegian–American subjects.

The Haugens were clearly comfortable in their lives as bilinguals and biculturals, and in their love of both America and Norway. They were ideal examples of bilingualism and biculturalism as it can be lived, as well as very fine scholars in their respective fields.

My first visit was followed by many others. Einar always asked me to come at 5 p.m. and it slowly dawned on me why. After about an hour of serious conversation, he would ask me if I wanted a Haugen special. The first time I asked him what it was and he said, "Martini with vodka on ice." I'm not a hard alcohol drinker but I accepted and it was indeed very nice; we continued our chat, often with Eva with us, and another Haugen special would appear. By the time I got back home, I told myself there was some truth to the fact that Scandinavians like a good drink. This said, each time I came away, I felt more confident in the work I was doing and more serene as a bilingual and bicultural person myself. These visits had a very real impact on my career and on my life. Einar Haugen was just the kind of person a young author needed: he took me under his wing, was very supportive, gave me advice, and read every chapter of my future book.

Many years later, in 2016, I was asked to give the yearly Einar Haugen lecture at the University of Oslo. I entitled it, "Understanding the bilingual individual: Extending Einar Haugen's work," and I presented many ideas he had had, and proposals he had made, that I went on to extend. For example, he opposed the view, as did the Berkeley researcher Susan Ervin-Tripp, that bilinguals change personality when they change language. I extended what they said by stating that what is seen as a change in personality is most probably simply a shift in attitudes and behaviors that correspond to a shift in situation or context, independent of language.

Writing my book

The preparation and writing schedule I gave myself for my book was strict. For each chapter, there were two months of preparation and one month of writing. The latter took place early in the morning (from 4.00 to 7.00) in the MIT student library, the only library I knew of that was open at night. This allowed me to then have a regular day at Northeastern, teaching and doing my research. I kept to this schedule—it was a bit like all that cross-country running in my adolescence which required a lot of perseverance—and I finished the book in sixteen months. I wrote every chapter in longhand (I have kept a few manuscript pages from back then) and then had them typed. This was just a few years before the onset of word processing. I handed in the manuscript in the early summer of 1981 and the book was published in July 1982.

The book contained six rather long chapters with very different themes: bilingualism in the world, in the United States, and in society; the bilingual child, the bilingual person, and bilingual speech and language. I discussed the political and social situations that arise when languages come into contact, and the policies that nations have established toward their linguistic minorities in the domains of education and governance. I spent a lot of time on the psychological and social factors that lead a bilingual to choose one of her languages when speaking to another bilingual, or use both languages through code-switching and borrowing. I also explained how children become bilingual as quickly as they revert back to monolingualism if two languages are no longer needed. In addition, I described the organization of the languages in the bilingual brain researched through the study of polyglot aphasics or with experimental tasks. Finally, I examined the legacy of bilingualism and wrote at the end of the book, "As long as languages continue to come into contact with one another, through individual bilinguals and in bilingual communities, they will not fail to influence one another. Language borrowing is the legacy of those who live with two languages."

Although I was writing a general and comprehensive introduction to the field, I wanted the book to also reflect the bilingual's point of view. I wanted those who lived with two or more languages to come through, just as Einar Haugen had done in his own writings. As I wrote in the Introduction: "Too much has been written by people who see the topic through the eyes of monolinguals." So I included many first-hand accounts from bilinguals and inserted them in "Bilinguals speak" boxes. I told readers that bilinguals tell about their experiences: how they use their two (or more) languages, their attitudes towards bilingualism, their educational experiences, their feeling about code-switching and language borrowing, and the differences they feel exist (or do not exist) between themselves and monolinguals.

Here are a few examples. In this first extract (p. 28), Cesar Chavez, the labor leader, talks about the monolingual education he received:

"In class one of my biggest problems was the language. Of course, we bitterly resented not being able to speak Spanish, but they insisted that we had to learn English. They said that if we were American, then we should speak the language, and if we wanted to speak Spanish, we should go back to Mexico."

In this next extract, the hearing daughter of a deaf American talks about her father (p. 86):

"My father is a union carpenter. Although a master carpenter, he's never been promoted to foreman even though he's worked fifty years in the trade. He said to me, 'You know, I'll never be a foreman because I'm not hearing.' "

And here, an Arabic–English bilingual explains how he rejected his home language, Arabic, in his youth (p. 163):

"As an adolescent I pretended I did not know Arabic, and I tried very hard to lose my foreign accent. I did this because I wanted very badly not to be any different from the rest of my friends. As I got older, though, I started to learn and appreciate my native languages and culture much more."

I have often been told that these first-hand accounts add something special to the book.

The book title that was on my contract, "Bilingualism in the World," was not eye-catching, I thought, and did not reflect the fact that using two or more languages in one's everyday life is as natural to the bilingual as using only one language is to the monolingual. According to me, bilingualism is neither a problem nor an asset but quite simply a fact of life. So I thought about a more appropriate title over several months and finally found one as I was walking to meet Lysiane at a restaurant in Harvard Square in Cambridge. When I arrived, I tried it out on her, "Life with Two Languages: An Introduction to Bilingualism." She liked it lot and I adopted it. Harvard University Press then had to be convinced but it wasn't too difficult as my copy-editor, Peg Anderson, understood exactly what it was that I wanted to do.

When I went to get my first published copy of the book at the Press on July 12, 1982—I still remember that day perfectly—I was amazed how big the book was; it first came out as a hardback and covers were thick in those days, as was the paper it was printed on. Only two weeks later we left for a year in Switzerland (see the next chapter), so I didn't see how it was initially received in the stores, but I was kept informed on how it was doing. Much to my surprise—I was a newcomer to the book publishing world—it got very good reviews and it has sold very well (some 26,000 copies since it first came out).

10

The children become bilingual

I stated in an earlier chapter that Cyril, our first son, had quickly become a dormant bilingual during our first year in the United States, and that we didn't worry too much about it as we thought we wouldn't be staying that long. His French would be reactivated in no time once we got back to France, we told ourselves. But we stayed on and our little Cyril never went back to French. Four years after our arrival in the States, Pierre, our second son was born and we hoped that with him we would do things right and make a real bilingual out of him. We made sure to speak French to him and we read him stories in French. However, from birth, he was also in contact with English through his brother, his brother's friends, his brother's TV programs, and finally at daycare. For the first few months of language learning, Pierre spoke both French and English and I remember proudly posting his new words in each language on my lab's notice board. But Pierre quickly realized, like his brother four years before, that he really only needed to use one language and that, for reasons related to school and to life outside the home, it had to be English. So he too slowly became monolingual in English. I reflected this when I dedicated my *Life with Two Languages* to my wife, Lysiane, and to our two sons, "for their monolingualism, so categorical and yet so natural."

A Journey in Languages and Cultures. First edition. François Grosjean.
© François Grosjean 2019. First published 2019 by Oxford University Press.

All this happened before I started reading widely, for my course and my first book, about how to make children bilingual and how to keep them that way. Had I known back then what I know now, we would certainly have done things differently. I have now written a number of posts on this issue for my blog, one of them aptly entitled, "Planned bilingualism: Five questions to consider".[1] There are a number of strategies parents can use, and there are ways of creating a real need for each language. As I write in the post, "It has long been known that children acquire languages, but also forget them, in a very short time depending on the need they have for each language: the need to communicate with family members, caretakers, or friends, to participate in the activities of a daycare or a school, to interact with people in the community, etc. If children feel that they really need a particular language, and other psychosocial factors are favorable, then they will develop that language. If the need disappears or isn't really there (e.g. the parents also speak the other language but pretend they don't), then the language may no longer be used and, over time, it may be forgotten."

One lesson I learned first-hand is that bilingual parents are not a guarantee that their children will be bilingual. The latter are very pragmatic and will not acquire a weaker language, often the minority language, unless the conditions are right. In addition, our own boys simply didn't receive enough French input from us and from other French-speaking caretakers, friends, family members, etc. to foster their bilingualism. After eight years in the United States, we had become a bilingual family in that two languages were spoken in the home, English and French. However, only we, the parents, were in fact bilingual; the two children were basically monolingual in English with very little comprehension of French. The language we used as a couple was French, but we did find ourselves at times speaking to one another in English, such as when the four of us were together and we wanted to make sure that the children understood what we had to say.

A sabbatical year in Switzerland

When we started considering where we would spend my sabbatical year in 1982–83, we thought immediately of a French-speaking country so that the children, who were now ten and almost five, could acquire French. In addition, we wanted them to get to see their French grandparents. They hardly knew them despite the fact that Lysiane's mother had come over to the States a few times and was even taking English lessons to be able to speak to them. France would have been the obvious place to go to but I was still on leave of absence, not with Vincennes precisely, but with the Foreign Affairs Ministry as a French civil servant abroad. It would have been difficult therefore to negotiate a sabbatical whilst still on leave.

So we fell back on Switzerland, a country I had lived in as a child, and a place we had returned to on vacation. I had met a young Swiss researcher at Brandeis, Jocelyne Buttet Sovilla, a speech/language pathologist, and I wrote to her to ask her if she knew of any universities that would be interested in a course in psycholinguistics. She was part of the speech/language pathology program at the University of Neuchâtel and, through her, I obtained a lectureship there. Then, by means of further contacts, I also obtained courses to teach at the universities of Zurich and Basel. I came over a few months before our move, met two future colleagues at the university (René Jeanneret and Bernard Py) and organized everything: a furnished apartment in a small village just outside Neuchâtel, a second-hand car waiting for us in a garage, a place in the village school for Cyril, and a slot in the local kindergarten for Pierre. Their final enrollment would take place a little later. I even brought back a few bottles of the local white wine.

We arrived in Paris in early August and stayed a few days in France before driving down to Switzerland with Lysiane's parents. I asked Cyril what struck him the most (I kept a diary throughout our year abroad and a bit beyond) and his first comments were: people speak a different language, the cars are not the same, people dress differently, the food is better... and the toilets are not in the bathroom but in a separate location. Our own first reactions were slightly different, eight years after having left: the streets were narrow and crowded, the cars drove too fast, were too close to one another, and didn't let you cross even if you were on a zebra crossing, people looked so serious and worried, and they didn't smile much. We had brought our smiles with us and we noticed that people looked at us strangely probably asking themselves, "Why is that person smiling like that?"

We arrived in our little village near Neuchâtel a few days later, and even before school started, Cyril had made friends. He saw kids his age playing in the village square, around the fountain, and he joined them. Because he was American, at least culturally, and was fun to be with, Cyril was an immediate success. His French at the start was nonexistent and his friends' English was no better so for a few weeks he used body language, a bit of English here and there, and a big smile. He also acquired a few short set expressions of the type, "Qu'est-ce que c'est?" (What is it), "Attention, s'il vous plaît" (Careful please) or "Il est gentil" (He's nice) which he'd utter along with gestures.

His new friends, in turn, did all they could to help him out. One of the ways was to simplify their French considerably. At the local village fair, for example, kids could "fish" for a present that an adult, behind a screen, would put on the hook. One of the prizes Cyril wanted was a rubber alligator. Knowing this, one of the French-speaking children said to Cyril in broken French: "Moi avoir alligator, te donner" (literally, "Me get alligator, I give you"). The sentence he would normally have used with a French-speaking friend would have been much more complex, of the type, "Si j'obtiens l'alligator, je te le donnerai." Cyril understood the simplified sentence and all was well but I'm not sure he ever did get the alligator.

Professor Lily Wong Fillmore from Berkeley stresses the importance of social processes whereby language learners have to make the speakers of the language aware of their needs, and get them to make accommodations and adjustments so that they can acquire the language. Cyril was helped a lot by these processes. For example, his teacher kept a French-English dictionary next to him to look up words and expressions to make sure Cyril would understand what he said. He also told him early on, "You'll learn French and I'll learn English!" Part of the school work was the weekly dictation (the infamous French "dictée") which, of course, Cyril could not do. So the teacher would give him the text in advance, and we would sit down and go over it word by word the evening before. His visual memory was amazing and the next day he would come home proudly stating that he had received full marks once again!

At the start of our stay, we were still an English-speaking family and when we went into Neuchâtel or to a public place like the local swimming pool, we all spoke English. This caused strange situations where some people we interacted with (e.g. salespersons) would speak to Lysiane and me in English, although we were both French speakers. So as not to have to explain that, yes, they were our children, and yes, we were French, but no, they didn't speak French, and then going into the reasons for this, we sometimes simply continued in English. On other occasions, our French might slip out and then we were complimented on speaking such good French for Americans.

Language learners can be very different from one another because of their age, cognitive abilities, personality, attitudes towards trying out new things, etc., and this will have an impact on how they acquire a second language. Cyril and Pierre are good examples of this. Cyril was a very outgoing, let's-try-it kind of boy, and he acquired broken French very quickly. He would make pronunciation errors, gender errors, grammatical errors, but he wouldn't mind, and he just kept communicating with his friends. Pierre was much more reserved and quiet and he used a different approach. For about three months he hardly said a word in French, either to his schoolmates or to his teacher. Instead he used a lot of body language and let the teacher use her basic English with him. He was busy acquiring the language, however, and he would show us what he knew when he came home: songs, rhymes, set expressions, etc. And when he did start to speak French freely, it was much more error free than Cyril's French. It was as if Pierre had let the language settle in and then, once everything was in place (grammar, pronunciation, vocabulary), he set about speaking the language. He even had the nerve to correct his older brother at times. For example, the latter said "formage" one day instead of "fromage" (cheese), and much to Cyril's annoyance, Pierre butted in and said, "C'est fromage, Cyril!"

Of course, both Cyril and Pierre's English intruded in their French. For example, speaking to his grandfather, Cyril said, "Ca c'est un <u>magnet</u>!" (That's a magnet). Watching a soccer game, he exclaimed, "Quel <u>faker</u>!" (What a faker). He would also code-switch with us, into either language, as in: "That's all I want *pour commencer* (to start)." And very quickly, when speaking to one another, the boys realized they could switch into French to catch the other's attention. I once heard Cyril tell Pierre, "Viens, viens!" (Come, come) before continuing in English. That said, they remained as happy and as mischievous as before; the only difference was that they talked and teased one another in "Franglais" and no longer only in English. Both children would reflect, from time to time, on their languages, a well-known effect of childhood bilingualism. Pierre one day told his parents, "I can't speak Chinese yet, because I've never been to China, but I could speak all the languages in the world... (pause)... but it would take a long time to travel around the world"!

While Cyril and Pierre were busy learning French and getting used to their new schools, Lysiane and I were slowly adapting to a new culture. Even though we knew Switzerland as tourists (my stay at Aiglon in my youth did not really count as my everyday environment was Anglo-American), we were now living there and were faced with many new things to get used to: stores closing at midday and ending their day at around 6 p.m., incredibly short kindergarten hours for Pierre, kids coming home for lunch, etc. Even small things like greetings were so different. People passing by whom we didn't know would say, "Bonjour," to us. So we tried it too but sometimes we were met with blank stares. Once, when I phoned the hockey coach for the first time, I said "Bonjour" and then told him why I was phoning (Cyril wanted to play hockey). He cut in abruptly and asked me to present myself. I quickly learned that in Switzerland, when on the phone, you give a greeting and then you introduce yourself, e.g. "Monsieur Grosjean à l'appareil" (Mr. Grosjean on the phone). You can then say why you are phoning.

When talking to Swiss acquaintances who were critical of the US, we found ourselves defending Americans and the American way of doing things. And we missed our lives in Cambridge/ Boston. As I wrote in my diary: "Last night, I had the same feeling as eight years ago when we arrived in the States: What am I doing here even though everything is so nice: the lake, the houses, the vineyards, the little villages, the mountains...? Here, although the environment is very pretty, it is also strange in the sense that it is not ours. We are strangers here. It is interesting that one needs another country and culture to start realizing and accept-ing who one is." A bit later I wrote, "Although we felt slightly foreign in the States, of all three countries—US, Switzerland, France—it is the one where we feel most at home. Our trip to Europe has made us realize how much we are rooted there."

But a few months later, things had calmed down and I wrote: "It is interesting how one goes through stages when one moves to a new country. First there is the newness and the excitement of the discovery (this lasted about two months). Then there is the backlash, the 'What am I doing here?' question. This is marked by a lot of letter writing back home and talk about how great it is back there (our third month here). Now we are in the third stage—we are settled down, the kids like it and are quasi-integrated, we have our teaching (Lysiane taught English) and we are slowly getting to know people. So now, we are accepting our stay and feel less in need for contact from the US."

My teaching in Neuchâtel, Zurich, and Basel went well although I was surprised by how silent the Swiss students were. They interacted far less with the lecturer than in the States and were not used to having a responsive lecturer who really cared about how much they understood. It was only at the end of the academic year that they opened up, told me how much they had enjoyed my teaching, and asked me why I was leaving.

On the family front, our year in Switzerland was soon over and we started saying goodbye after a final trip to the South of France. Our family language had switched over to French, and from being a French couple with two monolingual English-speaking children, we had become a totally French-speaking family. Cyril spoke very fluent French but it was basically conversational and he did not write it very well. As for English, he had maintained it but spoke it with a few hesitations and some mixing. Pierre, on the other hand, was on the verge of becoming a French mono-lingual; he never spoke English and had a hard time repeating simple English sentences.

Keeping their bilingualism alive

We returned to the United States in August of 1983. After an eight-hour flight, the use of French suddenly became restricted to one domain—the home. English took over again and Cyril switched over in no time. It took Pierre a bit longer but about twelve days after our return, coming back in the car with Cyril and a friend, he suddenly said about the cake we would eat back home: "It's not a cake, it's an ice-cream cake." His English was back!

Our struggle to keep French "alive and well" in our children was about to start. Lysiane and I decided we would do everything we could to maintain our children's French, not only because it would be a pity to see it disappear when it had been "picked up" so easily, but also because it had taken on certain sentimental values. The children could now speak directly to their grand-parents without using us as interpreters, they had friends in

Switzerland they would see again, and we could speak to our own children in our native tongue.

We used several approaches to maintain their French. We insisted that French be the home language, and that all activities at home take place in French. This was easier said than done because English entered the home with school friends, home work, the television, neighbors, etc. But on the whole the strategy worked quite well and French was indeed the home language. We also attempted to find French-speaking friends for our children. We were constantly on the lookout for French-speaking children who had just arrived in the Boston area and who were still monolingual. This strategy was a very good one when the children got along together (which was not always the case) as French was the natural language of communication between them. Of course, after a few months, the newcomers had acquired some English and the interactions often took place in both languages or in English. But for a while, at least, our children used French with their peers.

We also invited Cyril and Pierre's French and Swiss friends to the United States. These young boys were thrilled to come over for three or four weeks, and the parents were often prepared to pay for the flight; we took care of the rest. As one might suspect, these children knew almost no English, and thus Cyril and Pierre had to interact with them in French. The whole thing took place very naturally, much more so than with bilinguals like us. The additional advantage was that Cyril and Pierre were invited, in turn, to their friends' home that same year or the year after. Finally, we saved up for a trip to Europe once a year. This allowed the children to use their French in all domains of life and to be back in the "ambiance" they had discovered in Switzerland. Three years later, in the last entry in my diary, I wrote that both boys used French quite naturally and were well on the way to keeping it for good.

This is how I ended my chapter on "Family strategies and support" in *Bilingual: Life and* Reality:[2] "Becoming bilingual and bicultural should be a joyful journey into languages and cultures. When children undertake it, it is important that they be accompanied, if at all possible, by caring and informed adults who will ease their passage from one stage to the next, and with whom they can talk about what they are experiencing. When they have that kind of support, there is every chance that the bilingualism and biculturalism attained will be a success." As parents, Lysiane and I are proud to have helped our sons become bilingual. Both are in their forties, now, and Cyril uses three languages on a regular basis. As for Pierre, he knows five languages and uses four daily!

11
Reflections on the bilingual and the bicultural person

Once *Life with Two Languages* was finished and had been published, I realized that I had given a lot of space to the views of others in the book, as was proper since it was a textbook. My own views on bilingualism and on biculturalism, however, had perhaps not come through clearly enough and so I started thinking about writing more theoretical papers expressing them. I worked on them whilst I was on sabbatical in 1982–83 and continued doing so when I was back at Northeastern.

The bilingual is not two monolinguals in one person

My thoughts on the bilingual person came out in 1985 with the title, "The bilingual as a competent but specific speaker-hearer".[1] A very similar version, "Neurolinguists, beware! The bilingual is not two monolinguals in one person",[2] to which I added implications for the neurolinguistic study of bilingualism, most notably aphasia, appeared a few years later. It is the second part of the latter's title, "The bilingual is not two monolinguals in one

A Journey in Languages and Cultures. First edition. François Grosjean.

person," that has been repeated by colleagues over and over again in books, chapters, articles, and even blog posts for practically thirty years.

Both papers underline that a monolingual (or fractional) view of bilingualism has been prevalent—and still is among some people—when we talk about those who use two or more languages (or dialects) in their everyday lives. According to a strong version of this view, the bilingual has (or should have) two separate and isolable language competencies; these competencies are (or should be) similar to those of the two corresponding monolinguals; therefore, the bilingual is (or should be) two monolinguals in one person. This monolingual view of bilingualism has had a number of consequences. One of them is that bilinguals have been described in terms of the proficiency and balance they have in their two languages. The "real" bilingual has long been seen as the one who is equally, and fully, proficient in two languages. He or she is the "ideal," the "true," the "balanced," the "perfect" bilingual. All the others—in fact, the vast majority of bilinguals—are "not really" bilingual.

Another consequence is that language skills in bilinguals have almost always been appraised in terms of monolingual norms. The evaluation tools used with bilinguals are often quite simply those employed with the monolinguals of the two corresponding language groups. These assessments rarely take into account the bilinguals' differential needs for their two or more languages or the different social functions of these languages, i.e. what a language is used for, with whom it is used and where (what I have since called the Complementarity Principle). The results from these tests invariably show that bilinguals are less proficient than the corresponding monolinguals. People then talk of "a bilingual disadvantage" instead of "a bilingual difference." I maintained then, and still do, that monolingual tests are, for the most part, inappropriate to evaluate the language skills of bilinguals.

A further consequence is that the contact of the bilingual's two (or more) languages is seen as accidental and anomalous, at least by lay people. Because bilinguals are (or should be) two separate monolinguals in one person, covert or overt contact between their two languages should be rare. The two language systems should be autonomous and should remain so at all times. If there is contact, it is accidental and is simply the result of language interference. Mixing languages in the form of code-switching or borrowing is still seen by some as the product of "shoddy" or "negligent" language when, in fact, it is a perfectly normal bilingual behavior when bilinguals who share the same languages communicate among themselves.

One last consequence of the monolingual view, something that has always saddened me, is the fact that bilinguals themselves often criticize their own language competence: "Yes, I use English every day at work, but I speak it so badly that I'm not really bilingual" or "I mix my languages all the time, so I'm not a real bilingual," or even, "I have an accent in one of my languages so I'm not bilingual." Other bilinguals strive their hardest to reach monolingual norms, and still others hide their knowledge of their "weaker" language(s).

On a personal level, my lifelong observations of bilinguals, and my reflections on my own bilingual behavior with monolinguals and with bilinguals, convinced me that bilinguals are neither better nor worse than monolinguals but are different communicators. I was fully aware of speaking just one language in certain situations, and mixing my two languages in others. I was also conscious that as I changed language dominance over time due to my migrations, and as I acquired but also forgot some languages

(Italian, American Sign Language), I remained the same human communicator although my linguistic needs evolved and hence my linguistic profile changed.

It dawned on me that the best way to talk about, and study, bilinguals and bilingualism should be in a holistic manner. Thus, in those two papers, I proposed that bilinguals are NOT the sum of two complete or incomplete monolinguals; rather, they have a unique and specific linguistic configuration. The coexistence and constant interaction of the two or more languages in bilinguals has produced a different but complete language system. The analogy I used comes from the domain of track and field. Hurdlers blend two types of competencies—that of high jumping and that of sprinting—into an integrated whole. When compared individually with sprinters or high jumpers, hurdlers meet neither level of competence, and yet when taken as a whole, they are athletes in their own right. No expert in track and field would ever compare hurdlers to sprinters or high jumpers, even though the former blend certain character-istics of the latter two. In many ways, bilinguals are like hurdlers: unique and specific communicators.

Apart from a few exceptions, such as translators and inter-preters, for whom I later used the label "special bilinguals," bilinguals use their two (or more) languages, separately or together, for different purposes, in different domains of life, with different people. Because the needs and uses of the two languages are usually quite different, bilinguals are rarely equally and completely proficient in their two or more languages. Levels of proficiency in a language will depend on the need for that language and will be domain specific.

It is in these papers that I stated that language use should be the main variable put forward in the definition of the terms "bilingualism" and "bilingual." I wrote that bilingualism is the regular use of two (or more) languages, and that bilinguals are those people who need and use two (or more) languages in their everyday lives. (I added dialects to languages in my definition later on). Although proficiency is not mentioned in the definition, it is implicit as one cannot use a language without having some level of proficiency in it.

A number of other important concepts are mentioned in these papers, often for the first time. Over the following years, I was to give them a more definite form in my writings. The Complementarity Principle, mentioned in several places, was also discussed when I dealt with language tests used with bilinguals. These rarely take into account the fact that bilinguals use their languages for different purposes, in different domains of life, with different people.

The concept of language mode was also clearly specified for the first time when I wrote that in their everyday lives, bilinguals find themselves at various points along a situational continuum which induce a particular language mode. In the monolingual language mode, the bilingual adopts the language being used (often that of a monolingual interlocutor) and deactivates the other language(s). In the bilingual mode, the bilingual speaker chooses a base language, activates the other language, and calls on it from time to time by code-switching or borrowing. In code-switching there is a complete shift to the other (guest) language for a word, a phrase, or a sentence. As for borrowing, a word or short expression is taken from the other language and is adapted morphologically, and often phonologically, into the base language. Borrowing can also involve simply taking the meaning of a word from another language and adding it to that of a word in the base language. In sum, code-switching is the juxtaposition of two languages whereas borrowing is the integration of one language into another.

Two other important phenomena had their roots in these two papers. The first concerned the waxing and waning of languages in bilinguals. New situations, new environments, new interlocutors will involve new linguistic needs in one language, in the other, or in both simultaneously, and will therefore change the language configuration of the person involved. After a period of readjustment, which can be more or less long and which may lead to a change in dominance, bilinguals will normally meet their new communicative needs as required. I have personally changed dominance four times in my life due to frequent migrations—from France to Switzerland and then England as a child, back to France as a young adult, to the United States in my late twenties, and to Switzerland when I was forty. I went through language restructuring each time, and after a few years my bilingualism stabilized. The other phenomenon concerns the assessment of young bilingual children which must try to tease apart whether they are still in the process of becoming bilingual or in a period of readjustment, whether they are normally in a bilingual language mode and have not yet discovered monolingual versions of the languages, or whether they are in fact meeting their communicative needs in the home environment and are just starting to acquire formal language skills required in school.

In the last part of these papers, I evoked possible impacts a holistic view will have on research: the study of how bilinguals structure and use two or more languages, separately or together, to meet their everyday needs; the development of tests that are appropriate to the domains of language use, monolingual in some instances, and bilingual in others; the controlling for language mode when running bilingual participants in studies; the distinction that needs to be made between those who are in the process of becoming bilingual and those who have reached a more or less stable level of bilingualism; and, more generally, the study of bilinguals as such and not always in relation to monolinguals.

I am happy to say that the holistic view I proposed at that time, and have defended ever since, has influenced many of my colleagues. Here are just a few that come to mind: Vivian Cook who studies the multi-competence of second-language learners and bilinguals;[3] Madalena Cruz-Ferreira who has researched, among other things, multilingual norms in the evaluation of bilingual children and adults; Elizabeth Peña and Lisa Bedore who have worked on the assessment of lexical and semantic knowledge of bilingual children; and Ofelia García who has done a lot of work on translanguaging in the classroom with bilinguals.

Describing the bicultural person

During my sabbatical in Neuchâtel in 1982–83, I also worked on what it means to be bicultural. I had hardly touched on the topic in my *Life with Two Languages* and yet it concerns many bilinguals who lead their lives in two or more cultures. And so I published my first article in French in the journal *Pluriel*,[4] and it is only much later that I took up most of what I said there in my books, *Studying Bilinguals*, and *Bilingual: Life and Reality*.

Bicultural people are characterized by at least three traits. First, they take part, to varying degrees, in the life of two or more cultures. Second, they adapt, at least in part, their attitudes, behaviors, values, etc. to these cultures. And third, they combine and blend aspects of the cultures involved. Certain characteristics such as beliefs, values, attitudes, behaviors, etc. come from one or the other culture whereas others are blends based on these cultures. Thus, contrary to bilingualism where it is possible to deactivate a language and only use the other in particular situations (at least to a very great extent), biculturals cannot always deactivate certain traits of their other culture(s) when in a monocultural environment. In my case, I certainly blend aspects of my four cultures, and in whichever culture I am in, they come through however hard I try to adapt fully to just one culture.

Contrary to general belief, bilingualism and biculturalism do not always go hand in hand. People can be bilingual without being bicultural (think of Europeans who use two or more languages in their everyday lives but who live in only one country and within one culture), and people can be bicultural without being bilingual such as British expatriates who have lived in the United States for many years. But of course, many bilinguals are also bicultural; they use two or more languages in their everyday lives and they navigate within and between their different cultures.

People can become bicultural at different points in time. Children can be born within bicultural families or come into contact with a second culture outside their home or in school, as was my case. Adolescents may pursue their studies in another culture and, of course, many adults emigrate to other regions or countries and slowly acculturate into their new culture (as my family and I did with the United States). It is important to note that the cultures involved rarely have exactly the same importance for the bicultural person; one culture often plays a larger role leading to cultural dominance, similar to language dominance in bilinguals. In addition, cultures can wax and wane in one's lifetime, become dominant for a while before taking a secondary role later on, and vice versa.

Bicultural people navigate along a situational continuum that requires different types of behavior: at one end they are in a monocultural mode since they are primarily with monoculturals. Here they have to deactivate as best they can their other culture(s). If their knowledge of the culture in question is adequate, and the deactivatation is sufficient, then they can behave in a monocultural way such as hold a meeting according to the rules of that culture, deal with monocultural business partners, welcome acquaintances, and so on. However, because of the blending component in biculturalism, certain attitudes, behaviors, feelings, etc. may not be totally monocultural. For example, my greeting behavior is not totally monocultural when I'd like it to be, despite my efforts to behave in the right way in each of my four cultures I interact with. When in England, I have a tendency to shake hands at the end of a visit when a small wave would be sufficient. Shaking hands takes place at the beginning of an encounter, usually, and is often not repeated at the end.

Greeting women friends with a kiss can also be problematic: who to kiss, and how many times. Should it be a brief air kiss as in the US, two kisses as in France, or three as in the French-speaking part of Switzerland? I usually do things right but it becomes more difficult when meeting a friend outside of their own culture, such as a Swiss friend in France. Does she expect two kisses because we are in France or three because we are both from Switzerland? Another example of the impact of cultural blending in a monocultural environment is how I attract a waiter's attention in a French café. I just can't bring myself to be quite as conspicuous as the normal French customer. Instead of saying, "Garçon!" with a loudish voice, I try to attract the waiter's attention through eye contact and by raising my hand meekly, which invariably leads to failure, at least for the first few tries. The blending component present in biculturals can be observed in many other ways such as in the hand gestures used, the amount of space one leaves between oneself and others, what one talks about, etc.

At the other end of the situational continuum, bicultural people are in a bicultural mode since they are with other biculturals who share their cultures. They use a base culture to interact in and bring in the other culture, in the form of cultural switches and borrowings, when they choose to. My colleague and friend, Aneta Pavlenko, gave me an example of Russian-American teenagers in Philadelphia who may spend Friday evening with their families laughing over a popular Soviet-era comedy and then go out on Sunday night together to see a new Hollywood blockbuster. They'll chat about the movie in English but slip in a few Russian adjectives or a reference to a popular character from a Russian movie. Biculturals often say that life is easier when they are with other people with the same bicultural background as them. They can relax and not worry about getting things right all the time. They often state that their good friends, or dream partners, are people like them, with whom they can be totally at ease.

A crucial aspect of being bicultural is coming to grips with one's identity. In Chapter 5, I described how difficult it was for me to figure out who I was when I returned to France after ten years in English boarding schools. I took into account how I was perceived by both the English and the French—the signals were contradictory (French for the English, English for the French)—and I then had to reach a personal decision, basing myself on my identity needs, my knowledge of the two languages and cultures involved, where it was I was living, etc. Of the four possibilities I had—identify with the English, identity with the

French, identify with neither, and identify with both—I chose the second solution. Choosing a French identity, even though I was in reality both French and English, was my way of trying to overcome the difficulties of readapting to my first culture. In general, opting for just one culture when bicultural is under-standable, and sometimes the best solution at a given time, but it does not really reflect the person who has roots in several cul-tures. Rejecting all cultures, on the other hand, or simply not facing the identity question, can lead to feeling marginalized or ambivalent. My identification solely with my French side came to an end in the United States where I felt accepted for who I was, both French and English. Then, with time, my English side became Anglo-American as I took on American traits. This soothed some of the bad memories of my years in England, and after a few years in the US, I accepted that I was in fact a mosaic of three cultures. As we will see, I then added a fourth culture when we settled permanently in Switzerland later on.

I stopped working on biculturalism—I am, after all, trained in the languages sciences and not in cross-cultural psychology—but I ventured back into the field when I started to reflect on the deaf as both bilingual and bicultural (see Chapter 8). Then, many years later, a colleague asked me to write a paper on bicultural bilinguals[5] and it is there that I managed to take up a number of themes that I had thought and written about over the years: how bicultural bilinguals are described in the literature, how they become both bilingual and bicultural, how their languages and cultures wax and wane over time, their linguistic and cultural behavior as bicultural bilinguals, how they identify themselves both linguistically and culturally, as well as their personality as bicultural bilinguals. Many of the things I stated can be found in various parts of this book but it might be worth citing the very last paragraph of the paper which stresses how important it is to study, in the years to come, both the linguistic and cultural aspects of bicultural bilinguals:

"The study of bicultural bilinguals from a linguistic and a cultural point of view, but also as unique entities, is a challenge for this century. Despite the fact that we are starting to understand the linguistic and the cultural components of these individuals, very little work has been done so far to describe the combined linguistic and cultural ensemble that is at the heart of who they are. Bicultural bilinguals are not simply the sum of two (or more) different languages, or of two (or more) distinct cultures. They have their own linguistic and cultural competence that is different from that of bilinguals who are not bicultural and from that of biculturals who are not bilingual. Hopefully descriptive, experimental and theoretical studies in the future will allow us to better appraise bicultural bilinguals as they are— complete and unique linguistic and cultural beings."

12

A difficult choice

Starting a research program on bilingualism

My sabbatical year in Switzerland in 1982–83 had allowed me to think and write about the bilingual and the bicultural person in what I hoped was an interesting and innovative way. It was also a time when I started planning a research program on bilingualism for when I returned to the United States. I was of the opinion that psycholinguistics needed much more work on the perception and production of language in the bilingual's different language modes: the monolingual mode, and the bilingual mode, i.e. when language mixing is taking place. It was important to describe the ways in which bilinguals in the monolingual mode differ from monolinguals in terms of perception and production processes, and explain the actual interaction of the two (or more) languages during processing in the bilingual mode.

Since there were already some studies that had examined bilinguals in a monolingual mode (although I have often questioned if they were indeed always in such a mode), I decided to concentrate my efforts on trying to understand the underlying processes that govern mixed language production and perception.

A Journey in Languages and Cultures. First edition. François Grosjean.
© François Grosjean 2019. First published 2019 by Oxford University Press.

I wrote up a large research grant which I submitted to the National Science Foundation entitled, "Language Processing in Bilinguals," and after a tense waiting period, I was awarded three years of funding. This allowed me to obtain extra office and laboratory space as well as additional equipment from my university, and to take on research assistants. A few months later, my department promoted me to full professor, a very real honor for someone who had arrived from abroad ten years before as a part-time assistant professor. I was 38 and academic life couldn't have been any better.

Judith Bürki, Jane Wozniak, Lysiane, and I worked on a number of perception and production studies over the next few years. We tested members of the European French community in the greater Boston region, some of whom we knew, others whom we met for the first time. What was original was that every experiment was portable: if some participants could not come to the laboratory, we would run the experiment in a quiet room in their homes. This worked very well and we obtained excellent data that way. Sometimes, if there were young children in the home, I would transform myself into a caretaker whilst their mom or dad was busy doing a study in another room. It was a step towards ecological experimental research before its time.

The studies we ran were quite varied. There was a "telephone chain" experiment to see how bilinguals changed their way of speaking when addressing different types of interlocutors— French newcomers in the US, bilinguals who were very careful not to mix languages, regular code-switchers, etc. We also did some more controlled studies to examine how code-switching takes place at the phonetic level, millisecond by millisecond. And on the perception side, we examined how guest words—one word code-switches as well as borrowings—were recognized by bilingual listeners, and how syllables, some of them intermediate between French and English, were perceived in different language contexts. Much of this work was written up and published in the following years and some of it encouraged others to pursue these topics further.

While this research was taking place, I also pursued studies with colleagues such as Jim Gee with whom we examined the importance of prosodic structure in monolingual word recognition, as well as narrative structure, and Joanne Miller who was interested in the influence of articulation rate on speech perception. And then there were the studies that I had started in Neuchâtel with colleagues there. Etienne Cornu, a young mathematician and computer scientist, had asked me if he could do a study with me for his Master's thesis. I was intrigued by the fact that Cyril, our eldest boy, kept telling us that people would constantly correct the gender mistakes he made (e.g. saying "le petit fille" instead of "la petite fille"). So I proposed to Etienne that we test whether gender marking on French articles (le/la, un/ une) helped French listeners recognize the following noun. If so, it could explain, in part at least, why Cyril's interlocutors reacted so noticeably to his use of the wrong gender. We did a gating study together and found that, indeed, gender marking plays an important role in noun recognition. A further study was done later with other colleagues and we then published the results.[1] It was one of the very first papers that examined this topic in spoken language processing.

The other study that I started in Neuchâtel, and continued working on when back in the United States, is worth mentioning as I later talked to Noam Chomsky about it. One of the professors who had welcomed me for my sabbatical was Bernard Py, an applied linguist who was interested in doing an experimental study with me. The question we asked was whether one's knowledge, or competence, of a first language could be changed when it is in contact over many years with a second language, even though the contact started when the person was an adult. So we asked first generation Spanish immigrants in French-speaking Switzerland, all of whom had been born in Spain and knew no French until age 20, to tell us if they accepted a number of Spanish grammatical variants influenced by French. All had lived in Neuchâtel for some twenty years and spoke both Spanish and French on a daily basis. For example, did they accept the French-influenced sentence, "El león quería morder el hombre" (The lion wanted to bite the man) when Spanish monolinguals would say, "El león quería morder al hombre"? Did they accept, "Decidió de llamar al médico" (He decided to call the doctor) when Spanish monolinguals would say, "Decidió llamar al médico"?

When we compared their results to those of monolingual Spanish speakers, we found that some of these new Spanish variants were accepted, to varying degrees, by our first generation immigrants. Of course, they still preferred the standard Spanish variants but they had made room in their Spanish language competence for some of the new variants. When I spoke about these results to Noam Chomsky (I'll return to our meeting below), his position was that the native language competence of the immigrants had not in fact been changed. Rather, it was their cognitive style that was now different. He suggested that when you move into a foreign language environment, your standards on grammatical acceptability are lowered because you are confronted with many ways of saying things, in the one or the other language, or in both. This change in cognitive style may thus explain the way you react to your native language, but it should not influence your knowledge of your native language.

In an attempt to get to the bottom of this, one of our students, Eliane Girard, moved away from acceptability judgments. She asked second generation Spanish–French bilinguals who had given similar acceptability judgments to those of the first generation participants, to interpret sentences into Spanish. Thus, for example, she got them to hear sentences such as, "Cet été nous allons en vacances en Espagne" (This summer we are going on vacation to Spain) and she recorded their interpretations. When she analyzed the results, she checked to see if they responded with, "Este verano vamos de vacaciones a España" (Standard Spanish variant) or "Este verano vamos de vacaciones en España" (Swiss-French Spanish variant).

What she found was that the rank ordering of the grammatical features influenced by French was the same as that found in the acceptability studies. Since interpreting is very different from making acceptability judgments, these new results would seem to speak against a simple change in cognitive style as suggested by Chomsky. The conclusion we came to at the end of these studies is that the impact of a second language over a lengthy period of time can be quite profound on the first language competence of adult native speakers. More specifically, we had found that the Spanish of native speakers who did not know any French before the age of 20 had been modified due to the long-term impact of French. And this change had also been found in the grammatical competence of the next generation several years later.[2]

Talking to Noam Chomsky about bilingualism

The meeting Noam Chomsky kindly accepted to have with me came as a result of my reading his book, *Knowledge of Language*, which came out in 1986. I was interested in finding out what he thought about bilingualism and how it fit into his thinking at the time. So I wrote to him and he very kindly accepted to see me. I had to wait several months though as the demand to see him was very high. Our exchange, which I recorded and then transcribed but never published, took place in his office in the now famous Building 20 at MIT. I was still a young academic at the time and I was touched that such an illustrious linguist would spend some time with me discussing a topic that had always intrigued me.

Noam Chomsky started off by saying that he knew very little about bilingualism but as our conversation continued, he clearly showed that he had given it some thought. He was not convinced that there is a sharp difference between monolingualism and bilingualism. As he stated: "I'm about as monolingual as you come, but nevertheless I have a variety of different languages at my command, different styles, different ways of talking, which do involve different parameter settings." I kept coming back to this first point throughout the interview (for me, bilinguals ARE different from monolinguals) and a bit later on, when I asked him whether shifting styles is really the same as shifting languages, he did add, "It's different in degree, very different, VERY different in degree, so different in degree that you could call it a difference of quality. Because, after all, degree differences do turn into quality differences." For Noam Chomsky, the really interesting question is how a particular system of the mind can be simultaneously in several different states, and whether this is unique to the language faculty. He believes that it isn't.

Another topic we spent some time on concerned whether you can lose a first language in adulthood. Noam Chomsky didn't think you could and argued that there is some sort of residual storage. He took the example of a 60-year-old man who hasn't spoken German since age 20 and who no longer seems to be able to use it. The real test for him would be to see how quickly he could relearn it. He was convinced that the person would learn German a lot faster than if he were starting from scratch and he added that he would probably learn it with the right pronunciation, the right nuances, and so on. As he stated, "My guess is that you can't really erase the system."[3]

Finally, I asked Noam Chomsky why linguists, most notably theoretical linguists, had spent so little time studying bilingualism. After all, wasn't half the world's population bi- or multilingual? He did not play down the interest of understanding people who know and use several languages but he thought that theoretical linguists should start with simple cases, that is with monolinguals. For him, the argument is the same as for chemists who study just H_2O and not other types of water that contain other substances. To understand the latter, you have to start with the former. As he stated, "The only way to deal with the complexities of the real world is by studying pure cases and trying to determine from them the principles that interact in the complex cases." This is taken for granted in the physical sciences, according to him, and it should also be in the non-physical sciences. Our meeting lasted about an hour and I came away with some answers but also additional questions and a few doubts. That said, I felt honored to have spent some time with one of the great thinkers of our time, and I still feel that way so many years later.

The mid 80s was also a time when I started venturing out of regular academic publishing circles and accepted requests to write for a more general audience. My very first attempt was an OpEd for *The Miami News* which appeared on January 2, 1986. I was asked for a piece which would counter one by Gerda Bikales, executive director of U.S. English, a Washington-based organization which advocates nationally for the primacy of the English language. I stressed in my piece that linguistic diversity is rarely the cause of strife between groups and that the more multilingual a nation is, the less likely a conflict will occur. I also claimed that the United States is a mosaic of cultures and a land of many languages, and that bilingualism in the country is basically transitional. Many migrants in the US, sometimes even within one generation, go from monolingualism in their native language to monolingualism in English. I regretted that a national resource—the country's knowledge of the languages of the world—was being wasted instead of being preserved. I ended with the statement that bilinguals are the intermediaries between language groups, the cement that hold a multilingual mosaic together, and that they should be fostered by all sides. Later in my career, I was to write many more OpEds explaining and encouraging bilingualism, as well as give interviews, both spoken and written.[4]

Which country to choose?

As mentioned earlier, we had kept many ties with friends and colleagues in Neuchâtel after our year there. Several had come over to visit us in the US and we returned every summer for several weeks. My Neuchâtel colleagues started talking to me about coming back for good and since Lysiane and I had never given up on the idea of returning to Europe, I started looking for positions there. I applied for a professorship at the University of Lausanne, went over to visit and give a talk, but did not get it in the end. I thought that I would have a better chance of finding something if I was in the country itself, so in late 1985 I asked my department at Northeastern for a one-year leave of absence starting in July 1986. That would give me some time to find some lectureships in Neuchâtel, Basel, and Zurich, since I would not be paid half my salary as I had been for my sabbatical.

At that precise time, I was offered a position at McGill. So there I was, with a professorship at Northeastern, an offer from McGill, and a leave of absence in Neuchâtel for a year. We finally decided to cross McGill off the list as we felt that relocating to Montreal would be too great a change for us and the boys. In the early spring of 1987, I was offered a full professorship in Neuchâtel and I accepted it. I then sent in a letter of resignation to Northeastern and a group letter to friends. Here is an extract taken from the latter: "After twelve years in the States, we are finally going back to Europe for good, and as you can all imagine, it is with mixed feelings. You cannot live in a country for so long without being attached to it, especially when your children are (still!) a perfect reflection of its culture. So many things, so many friends make us feel at home in the States. But at the same time, the call of Europe has never disappeared and we have finally answered it."

Many years later, I wrote an OpEd in support of America after the first year of the Trump Administration.[5] I started it this way, remembering those years spent over there: "The United States has many friends throughout the world but maybe none so close as those of us who lived within its borders for many years before moving on. This was my family's case at the end of the last century. We worked among you, acculturated to your way of living, discovered many new things, and made wonderful friends. Our children grew up with yours, went to your schools, and took part in your everyday activities. They were no different from those of families who had been there longer. When we departed after twelve years, with regret, we left part of our hearts with you.

But, we have kept in touch with colleagues and friends, whom we go back to visit or who come over to us. Despite the fact that we now live abroad, your news is still our news, your joys are our joys, and your concerns, our concerns."

In July 1987, we returned to Boston for three weeks to pack up and say goodbye. We also had to explain why we were leaving. One friend said, "But you've made it over here: you're a full professor, you have a grant, and a great research program. You're a success story. Why do you want to go back to Europe?" I replied, "You know, it's a bit like a Californian who has lived in Massachusetts for twelve years and finally decides to go back. No one really questions his decision. Well, it's not really any different in our case." We made sure to revisit all those wonderful places we had loved going to—Walden Pond, Cape Anne, Lexington— and we walked on those streets we knew so well, Mass Ave, Brattle Street, Belmont Ave...Then we said goodbye. In my diary, just before flying back to Europe, I wrote the following: "I love you America...I felt welcome by you and your people, but I couldn't see myself giving up my other side (Europe)...you marked me and I'll keep a very special place for you in my heart." That has been so to this day, some thirty years later.

13
Living and working in a fourth culture

Thirteen years after having moved to our third country, we were back in Europe for good. Not in France this time but in Switzerland. I thought I knew the country as I had spent six years of my youth there, had often been back on vacation, and had stayed two full years in Neuchâtel, first on sabbatical and then on leave. But visiting is definitely not migrating, and we had to get used to being immigrants in a new country.

Settling in

We had spent a year in a furnished apartment in 1986–87 and the very first thing we had to do now was to find a new home. We did this fairly easily in the same village outside Neuchâtel that had greeted us during our yearly stays. A few months after our arrival, I wrote the following to friends and colleagues in the States:

"There we were, like a young couple in our first home, at least our first Swiss home, with no furniture, no kitchenware, no linen . . . just a bunch of suitcases and two great kids. It reminded us of our arrival in the States thirteen years before. The only difference is that we were 'back immigrating'

A Journey in Languages and Cultures. First edition. François Grosjean.
© François Grosjean 2019. First published 2019 by Oxford University Press.

and had to start from scratch once again...Within a few weeks, and thanks to Ikea, we had beds, chairs, tables, etc. and just recently we have even bought a couch."

Our biggest concern, apart from my starting officially at the university, was making sure that both our boys would do as well as possible in their respective schools. Pierre continued going to the village school and found his friends from the year before. Cyril, on the other hand, was kept back a year at the local secondary school because he now had to take German lessons, something that all Swiss French kids are required to do quite early on, and that he had been exempted from the year before. He found German difficult, especially as he was already behind his peers, and it was only thanks to my new research assistant, Nathalie Kübler, and her mother, Christine, a second-language teacher and teacher trainer, that he started catching up. They spent quite a bit of time with him the first two years, explaining the intricacies of German and making sure he understood what he was asked to do in school.

There was also the problem of French now that both boys were regular school kids, and not just visiting pupils. This is what I wrote in a group letter to friends that first year:

"They both have problems with written French, a language so different from the spoken version, and sometimes so arbitrary that you end up believing that it was developed to trap the children of immigrants, as well as their parents. In fact, as is well known, the ability to write French correctly has long been a passport into the higher spheres of society. Cyril and Pierre's teachers often forget they have two young foreigners in front of them, what with their fluent spoken French and a name like Grosjean."

As parents, Lysiane and I spent a lot of time helping both boys with their homework and the subjects they found difficult.

Lysiane, as the native French speaker, concentrated on written French and the intricacies of formal style and correct grammar, whilst I became the French and Swiss history helper. We also found ourselves explaining cultural differences between the States, their home country, and Switzerland. We realized that the transition between living in the US and living in Switzerland would have its hard moments, as it would for us too, and so we did everything we could to smooth the process. That said, we knew that it was simply a question of time before we felt at ease in our new home. In the meantime, we kept in touch with friends in the States, invited several over, and went back in the summer quite frequently. We were also glad to be back in Europe, less than an hour away from the French border, and happy to be near Lysiane's parents in Paris. We started going up to see them several times a year, and they came down to see us as well.

A very different culture

It is amazing how a country open to the world in so many ways—industry, commerce, higher learning, tourism, etc.—and seemingly easy to understand, is in fact much more complex than one would think. Switzerland is a true federation where each canton (state) retains many prerogatives, education being one of them. It is also, because of its make-up, a country of constant compromise, at all levels. There is a permanent quest, often not noticeable, to find an equilibrium that takes into account the cantons, the languages, the religions, the political parties, and so on. We discovered all of this with time, as we did the very real cultural differences between the French-speaking part of Switzerland and the German-speaking part. The French-speaking Swiss obtain a lot of their news, literature, the arts, music, etc. from France, but do not actually identify with the French. They feel closer to the Swiss Germans in certain ways, although the majority do not speak German very often (even less so, Swiss German). They do not travel to the German-speaking part of Switzerland frequently, even though it is such a small country, and even less to the Italian-speaking part. Thirty years after our arrival, I still marvel at this political and cultural union that is an example of federalism and democracy the world over.

Of course, it's the little things in life that strike one as different at first. We had started to get used to how things are organized during our previous stays and continued to do so: work days start very early, as do schools, lunch is usually eaten at home with the children, the stores close early, and are rarely open on Sundays, and so on. We also had to become accustomed to the unwritten rules of social behavior in urban areas such as the strict rules concerning cleanliness and noise. For example, gardening cannot take place later than 8 p.m. and never on Sundays. As for interacting with people—neighbors, sales people, city employees, bus drivers, etc.—a certain level of formality is a must with the use of "Monsieur" and "Madame" being prevalent. You cannot go up to one of these people with a smile and simply say the equivalent of, "Hi . . . I'd like to . . . " It took us time to get to know people well and be on friendly terms with some of them, and in general we found them much more reserved than in the US and not as ready to become friends. But when one breaks through that barrier, friendships often become longstanding.

I spent a lot of time at the university, setting up and running my laboratory (see the next section), and found that many of these cultural traits carried over into what I thought would be a more international, easy-going, academic atmosphere. What

I discovered instead was the kind of formality and distance I had experienced some twenty years before in Paris, at the Sorbonne, before May 68. My years at Vincennes and then in the US had been a break from this, and I had to get used to being more reserved, less outgoing, and more respectful of the social hierarchy that I found at the university. As a full professor, people expected me to reflect my social standing, to prefer being with my peers, and not be over-friendly with my assistants and my students. I found that I could be myself in my courses and seminars, and the feedback I received was good, but I had to be more formal on other occasions such as in meetings and during exam sessions.

An American-style laboratory

A very positive aspect of being a full professor in the Swiss university system is that you could run your unit, in my case a research laboratory, in a very independent way. The university had gone to great trouble to find me space which they refurbished entirely, and to buy me the equipment I needed (speech processing apparatus, computers, etc.), not to mention giving me a yearly budget to run the lab. I was appreciative of this, all the more so as it was the first laboratory of its kind in my college. My contract stipulated that I would teach and do research in psycholinguistics and phonetics, as well as natural language processing (NLP). The latter concerns such things as getting computers to understand written language, translate from one language to another, recognize human speech, as well as synthesize it. This was an interesting challenge that I set about meeting. I therefore named the laboratory, "Laboratoire de traitement du langage et de la parole" (Language and Speech Processing Laboratory), a title that covered both human and machine processing, and that involved written and spoken language. My first two research assistants were Nathalie Kübler, a linguist, and Alain Matthey, a computer scientist.

There was an American company at the time in Neuchâtel, Alps (Automated Language Processing Systems), that specialized in interactive translation systems. I was asked to interact with them, do joint projects if at all possible, and organize internships with them for our students. Because I was basically American-trained, and had just arrived from the US, we immediately got on well and my laboratory collaborated with Alps, and then their spin-off, Lexpertise Linguistic Software. The latter developed word-processing writing aid tools and, at first, we helped them by putting together computerized dictionaries and evaluating their tools.

Lexpertise closed down after a couple of years but our collaboration had given us a niche and we obtained a very large three-year grant from the CTI (originally CERS), the Swiss Confederation's funding agency for innovation, to work on the prototype of an English writing tool and grammar checker for French speakers. The writing and checking needs of non-native speakers writing in their second language are quite different from those of native speakers, many of the former's errors being directly linked to their first language. And so our prototype contained both writing aids (dictionaries, an on-line grammar, a verb conjugator, etc.) and two checking devices—a problem word highlighter which listed all the potentially difficult words in the text (false friends, confusions, etc.) and a grammar checker which detected and corrected morphological and syntactic errors. This project really marked the NLP research of the laboratory;[1] some eight researchers worked full- or part-time on it, and Etienne Cornu carried his part all the way to a Ph.D.

Other projects with outside partners involved the evaluation of various speech recognizers, speech synthesizers, and natural language interfaces to databases, as well as work for a local company on a phonetic keyboard for a speech communication aid for people with disabilities. One day I received a letter from a young lady who could not speak because of the developmental disorders she had suffered from. She had used this system with a head-mounted typing aid, and she thanked me for my help which had allowed her to communicate more fully. I was told by her mother that it had taken her a very long time to type the letter and I was extremely touched. I have kept it all these years as a reminder that linguistic research can sometimes have a profound impact on people's lives. It also reinforced my belief that as active researchers—if our research lends itself to it—we should be open to collaborating with applied fields.

On this front, we also developed a long-term partnership with the Lausanne University Hospital (CHUV) for which we did a number of projects for their aphasia unit and most notably with Jocelyne Buttet Sovilla. The first was to develop an identification and a discrimination test which involved the French phonetic /k/-/g/ continuum that ranged, in short steps, from the word "camp" (camp) to the word "gant" (glove). I did this work with my colleague and longtime friend from the University of Paris 8, Jean-Yves Dommergues. Our lab later developed for the CHUV— with the invaluable help of an electronics engineer, Daniel Varidel—a battery of on-line perception and comprehension tests for aphasic patients. Once the battery was finished, and had been evaluated at the CHUV, we distributed it to a number of aphasia centers in France.

Regular psycholinguistic research also took place in the lab. I'll come back to work on bilingualism in the next chapter but we also studied interesting aspects of French that make its perception and comprehension different from English. For example, we undertook a number of collaborative studies with Joanne Miller, a colleague at Northeastern University, and Jean-Yves Dommergues, researching vowel duration in both Parisian French and Swiss French. Duration plays a much more important role in the phonological system of Swiss French than it does in standard French and we wanted to see, among other things, if native speakers of Swiss French used durational differences in addition to spectral differences when identifying vowels.[2]

We started studying other topics at the word recognition level which, at first, were only worked on in Neuchâtel. For example, spoken French is characterized by liaison, that is the articulation of a consonant at the end of a word which is not normally articulated (e.g. "tes" pronounced /te/) but which is present if the next word starts with a vowel (e.g. "tes amis" is pronounced /tezami/). Another phenomenon is "enchaînement" (linking) where the consonant at the end of a word, always pronounced this time, is attached to the vowel of the next word, as in "petite" and "amie" (girlfriend) pronounced /pəti/ + /tami /which makes it indistinguishable from "petit tamis" (small sieve). We also examined the perception of two word utterances in which the schwa at the beginning of the second word is not pronounced because of resyllabification, as in "ma recherche" pronounced "mar cherche." The way I organized this research was to propose to students doing their M.A. thesis with me to take on one of these topics and do a pilot study. After they had defended their work, and if the results seemed promising, I would then propose to do a full-scale study with funded research. Several of the students were then hired as research assistants and a few even continued on to a Ph.D.

Since Neuchâtel University did not have a doctoral program in experimental psychology or cognitive science, I made sure that students who wanted to work with me took the necessary courses in psycholinguistics and phonetics as well as different seminar offerings that covered important research issues. I also offered a statistics course which evolved into a college level course open to other students, and I invited many colleagues from abroad to come to give talks and meet with my students. Some even stayed for several weeks for joint projects and my students could interact with them. This created links with laboratories abroad, notably in the US, and some Neuchâtel students actually spent time there.

As for the students' research projects themselves, I adopted the personal tutoring approach that Harlan Lane had used with me back in Paris. This apprenticeship format meant spending many hours discussing the aims of a study, designing it, choosing the right experimental procedure and material, preparing the stimuli, running the participants, agreeing on the data analyses to undertake, and doing the statistics, not to mention writing up the study. The cherry on the cake was when a study, or a set of studies, gave exceptional findings which could be published in peer-reviewed journals. I would then help students write a journal article, and I usually put their names in first place if it was based solely on their work. By the time I closed the laboratory, some twenty years later, I had used this advising approach with over 80 M.A. and Ph.D. students. It took a lot out of me but the positive feedback I obtained from most students who had been initiated in this way to the world of research was extremely gratifying.

Despite being a small laboratory, we had a good reputation, and I received requests from students from other universities to come and do their Master's thesis with me, many from the University of Basel. Without quite realizing it, I was furthering the good entente between the language regions of the country. By the time I closed down the laboratory in 2007, twenty years after its opening, I was proud of its statistics: twenty-eight joint projects with industry; ten multi-year research grants, many from the Swiss National Science Foundation; a total of over three million dollars in research money; twenty-four collaborators paid on soft money over the years, and seventy-one publications in various journals and in edited books. But above all, I had been able to help students take their first steps in research in psycholinguistics, phonetics, natural language processing, and bilingualism. This will remain my biggest accomplishment, in my mind, not to mention the fact that a few now have a career in one of these fields.

Delving further into the bilingual person

As I stated in the preceding chapter, I pursued with my collaborators and students in Neuchâtel the research on bilingualism which I had started at Northeastern. The National Science Foundation (NSF) in the States allowed me to finish working on the grant that I had obtained before leaving, and after that I got funding from the Swiss NSF to pursue this work. My research concentrated on bilinguals as speakers and listeners, and in addition to doing studies, I strove to develop further the concepts pertaining to them as well as model their behavior.

The bilingual speaker

A lot of research on the bilingual speaker had been descriptive up till then, and I wanted to bring the speaking bilingual into the lab. I have already mentioned the concept of language mode, that is the fact that bilinguals find themselves at various points along a situational continuum which induce a particular mode (see Chapter 11). As indicated briefly before, I set about finding experimental evidence for this with the "telephone chain" study

A Journey in Languages and Cultures. First edition. François Grosjean.
© François Grosjean 2019. First published 2019 by Oxford University Press.

I undertook. French–English bilinguals retold stories in French, or described pictures, to a number of French interlocutors who were described to them but were not present. There were three interlocutors: one was a newcomer to the US who didn't speak English very well, the second was competent in English but clearly did not like mixing languages, and the third was a regular language mixer. They were thus situated, in my participants' mind, at three different points on the language mode continuum. Would their behavior change as a function of the interlocutor they were addressing? This proved to be the case. With the interlocutor who did not know the other language well, i.e. English, they practically did not produce any code-switches. With the person who was an active bilingual but preferred not to mix, they restrained their code-switching. And with the regular language mixer, they code-switched freely.[1]

A University of Basel student, Sonia Weil, who did her Master's thesis with me, replicated this first study but used Swiss German–French bilinguals. She found in addition that if you are addressing a person in what you feel is the wrong language, either because the person does not understand it or because he/she prefers the other language, then you will not just bring in elements of the other language (code-switch) but you will switch languages completely. Another student, Paolo Caixeta, also did a study of this sort with Brazilian Portuguese–French bilingual speakers whose knowledge of French was either intermediate or advanced. He replicated the earlier results, i.e. more mixing with a bilingual interlocutor, but he also found that the speakers who had an intermediate level of French produced more guest elements than the participants with an advanced proficiency. Of course, many other factors have an impact on how much mixing takes place in a conversation and this is starting to be shown in experimental work in other laboratories.

I had also noticed that very few studies until then had examined the phonetics of code-switching. So Joanne Miller, at Northeastern, and I joined up and we asked whether the phonetic momentum of the base language in speech production carries over into the guest language and hence affects the beginning of code-switches. In other words, are code-switches slightly tainted, at least at their onset, by the main language being spoken. French–English bilinguals were asked to retell stories in English, in French with English code-switches, and then in French with no code-switches. Sprinkled throughout the stories were nouns that began with an unvoiced stop consonant and that were close homophones in the two languages, e.g. Tom, Carl, Paul, taxi, telephone (téléphone), etc. We measured the voice onset time (VOT, i.e. the interval of time between the release of the stop consonant and the onset of voicing) of the initial consonant of the monosyllabic proper nouns produced in the three conditions. We found that the participants, when speaking just one or the other language, made a clear difference between English and French VOT values. As for the English code-switch values, they were quite different from the French values and similar to the English values. We concluded that switching from one language to another involves a total change at the phonetic level.[2] Since then, other researchers have shown that how "clean" the onset of code-switches are may depend on a number of factors such as the bilingual speakers themselves and the language they are switching into.

The bilingual listener

Doing perception studies in the lab is much easier than doing production studies, and we did quite a few of these ourselves. One that I found particularly intriguing, and whose monolingual counterpart I have already mentioned, relates to the fact that listeners of languages that have gender—French, Italian and Spanish, for example—use gender marking on words before a noun to facilitate their access to it. Thus, on hearing "le joli..." (the lovely), with an indication of the masculine gender on "le," listeners are faster at perceiving the noun, "garçon" (boy), for example, than if they hear "leur joli..." (their lovely; "leur" is not marked for gender) before "garçon." With Delphine Guillelmon,[3] we asked whether late English–French bilinguals would also be sensitive to gender marking. They had learned French in school but it was only as adults, mostly because of immigration, that they had become regular users of French. We ran them in a naming study (e.g. they had to repeat "garçon" in the above example) and compared their results to those of early bilinguals who had started using both their languages in their early childhood.

As expected, the early bilinguals showed a gender marking effect, i.e. their responses were speeded up when the noun was preceded by a congruent gender marking and they were slowed down when it was incongruent. The real surprise came from the late bilinguals. They simply did not use the preceding gender marking when recognizing the following noun. They were totally insensitive to gender cues even though they themselves made very few gender errors in production. We hypothesized that there is probably a sensitive period to acquire a gender marking mechanism in perception and that late bilinguals, whose first language

146

(English) does not have gender marking, missed it and could not master it later on. Several later studies by others replicated our findings. A few others have shown that gender marking may exceptionally be used by late learners such as when specific tasks are employed, the sentence context is rich, and the bilinguals are highly proficient in the second language.

Much of my research at that time concerned the perception of mixed speech, that is speech that contains code-switches and borrowings. Several years before, with Carlos Soares,[4] we had confirmed, much to our surprise, that the processing of code-switched words takes slightly more time than base-language words. I was to name this the "base-language effect," i.e. the fact that in normal bilingual discourse, base-language units (phonemes, syllables, words) are favored over guest-language units, at least at their onset, since the base language is the language being processed primarily and is the most active. With two French–Italian bilingual students in the lab, Corinna Domenighetti and Dolorès Caldognetto, we asked how long the delay lasts after the code-switch is over. If it is carried through to the next word(s), then the bilingual listener may start falling behind the speaker, something that seems quite counterintuitive to all those who practice code-switching on a daily basis.

Highly fluent French–Italian bilinguals in Switzerland were asked to listen to a short sentence followed by a list of words as in, "J'ai entendu les mots aéroport, grenouille, sapin, collier" (I heard the words airport, frog, fir tree, collar). The participants had to repeat the word in the second position of the list, "grenouille" in this example. In the code-switching condition, the second word was replaced by an Italian word, which took the same amount of time to repeat as the French word in isolation. Thus, in the example above, "cena" (dinner) replaced "grenouille."

Corinna Domenighetti and Dolorès Caldognetto found once again a short switching delay when the Italian word replaced the French one. What is fascinating, though, is that when a second group of participants, similar to the first, were asked to repeat "sapin," the French word just after "grenouille"/"cena," the repetition times, in both conditions, were similar. This seems to show that the switching delay is short-lived. By the time the following word arrives in the sentence, any delay that might have occurred has been made up. Once again, other researchers have looked at this recently and have shown that various variables such as switching direction, and the proficiency one has in the switch language, may account for how long the delay goes on for.

The recognition of guest words—code-switches or borrowings—was also the object of much research in my laboratory. As part of my NSF grant, I had examined the role of a number of guest-word properties during word recognition.[5] I had presented French–English bilinguals with English guest words (e.g. "slash," "lean") preceded by a French neutral context, "Il faudrait qu'on..." (We should) and followed by a final phrase in French. For example, "Il faudrait qu'on *slash* tous les prix" (We should slash all the prices) or "Il faudrait qu'on *lean* contre le mur" (We should lean against the wall). The words were presented in segments of increasing duration from beginning to end, i.e. they were gated, and after each presentation, participants had to write down the word they thought was being presented, indicate their confidence rating, and say whether they thought the word was French or English.

I was able to show that words that were marked phonotactically as belonging to the guest language (e.g. "slash," "blot," where "sl" and "bl" are frequent in English but very rare in French) were recognized sooner than words not marked in this way. I also showed that words that had near homophones in the base language (e.g. English "knot" is a near homophone of French "note") were processed with more difficulty, although the frequency of occurrence of the two also played a role. Finally, I found that the way a guest word was said, i.e. as a code-switch (in English here) or as a borrowing (in French), had an impact on the narrowing-in process that takes place in the listener's mind during word identification. Code-switches which contain clear phonetic indications as to the language they belong to were easier to process than borrowings. A student in the lab, Markus Leuenberger, then showed, with Swiss German–French bilinguals, that two other variables also play a role: the density of code-switching before the critical word (a higher density speeds up recognition as the guest language's activation is higher), and a constraining semantic context before the word (the more constraint, the faster the recognition). Finally, Nicolas Léwy constructed a computational model of bilingual lexical access (BIMOLA) based, to quite a large extent, on a verbal model I had proposed.[6]

A final set of studies done in my lab were quite original. They concerned interferences, that is deviations from the language being spoken (or written) due to the influence of the other, deactivated, language(s). Although numerous books and articles have been written about the production of interferences, we know very little about how they are perceived by bilinguals. Yet the topic is worthy of interest since we can ask whether bilingual listeners are affected by them or whether they take them in their stride, since they too produce interferences from time to time. In addition, they can have access to the language not being processed at that point, unlike the monolingual listener, and hence can use it to understand the interference(s) that they are hearing.

Two of my students, Delphine Guillelmon and Nathalie Favre, studied this precise point, the former using a simple comprehension paradigm (participants answered questions after hearing a text) and the latter using a word monitoring task (participants listened for a target word, placed just after a critical point in a sentence, and pressed a reaction time key when they heard it). Both showed that bilinguals generally do better than monolinguals when faced with speech containing interferences, but the results depended on the types of interference heard. When a word had no transparent counterpart in the language being heard or when an idiomatic expression simply made no sense when translated literally from the other language, bilinguals did much better.

Stepping back a bit

During this period I also spent time reflecting on research methodology in the field of bilingualism, and I examined further some concepts that play a role in our understanding of the bilingual person. In 1998, for example, I published a paper on methodological and conceptual issues in bilingual studies.[7] In it I argued that because the field of bilingualism is still relatively new, studies in the linguistics, psycholinguistics, language development, and neurolinguistics of bilingualism have often produced conflicting results. I suggested that some of the difficulties encountered by researchers, and some of the diverging results they had obtained, could have been lessened, if not avoided, had close attention been paid to methodological and conceptual issues. Among those I covered were bilingual participants, language mode, stimuli and tasks, as well as models of bilingual representation and processing. I dealt with each issue in the following way: first I explained it; then I discussed the problems it caused, and, finally, I proposed tentative solutions. To better understand each issue, I took examples from descriptive and experimental studies of normal bilingual adults and children as well as bilinguals suffering from aphasia and dementia.

To illustrate what I did, let me examine the issue of participants here. I noted that some researchers still did not fully share the field's understanding of who bilinguals are. When studies obtained results that did not correspond either to the monolinguals of the one or of the other language, they expressed their surprise. This could have been avoided had they accepted a more holistic view of bilingualism which considers bilinguals as speaker-hearers in their own right. A consequence of this is that they do not have to give exactly the same results as monolinguals (see Chapter 11). I also argued that the factors that had been taken into account when choosing participants were sometimes insufficient or controversial. I mentioned one study by four eminent psycholinguists, Anne Cutler, Jacques Mehler, Dennis Norris, and Juan Segui, who tested a group of fluent and balanced bilinguals who had equally perfect command of their two languages. They found the results they obtained puzzling and so they decided to subdivide them into two groups according to their dominance (even though they reported these bilinguals knew both languages to the same high level). They tried various approaches, but still could not make their results fit the pattern they expected, and so they fell back on asking their participants to indicate which language they would choose to keep if they developed a serious disease and their life could only be saved by a brain operation which would have the unfortunate side effect of removing one of their languages.[8]

I found this approach questionable as their participants were bilingual precisely because they needed their two or more languages for their everyday life. But even more importantly, I questioned whether there was any validity in trying to assess language dominance in this way. If there wasn't, then their results could not be be replicated. And this is exactly what Anne Cutler's Ph.D. student, Ruth Kearns, found in her doctoral work. She used the same kind of highly fluent participants, broke them down into two groups with the same question, but simply could not replicate the earlier results. My paper has since been widely cited and so I am hopeful that it has had some impact on how one studies bilinguals.

Another piece of work I did during that period was a chapter on language mode,[9] a concept central to my thinking and that I have already mentioned in various parts of this book. I first gave a definition of language mode: the state of activation of the bilingual's languages and language processing mechanisms, at a given point in time. I then described language mode in more detail, spelling out the factors that influence it, and examining the impact it has on language behavior. I followed this by reporting on the existing evidence there was for language mode in bilingual language production, language perception, language acquisition, and language pathology. I then discussed language mode as a confounding variable and suggested ways of controlling it. I ended by considering research topics related to language mode such as assessment, processing mechanisms, highly language dominant bilinguals, and modeling.

Without going into the many aspects discussed in the chapter, I should maybe stress three points. First, I still read or hear colleagues saying that their participants were in an "English language mode," or in a "Spanish language mode," etc. Since language mode concerns the level of activation of two (or more) languages, one of which is the base language, two factors underlie the concept. The first is the base language chosen and the second is the comparative level of activation of the two languages, from very different in the monolingual mode to closer in the bilingual mode. Thus, one needs to indicate not only the base language but also the level of activation of the two languages. For example, a person can be in an "English bilingual mode" meaning that the base language is English and the other language is activated but less so than the base language. Or the person can be in a "Spanish monolingual mode," indicating that Spanish is the base language and the other language is not activated. Simply saying that a bilingual is in an English language mode leaves totally open whether the mode is monolingual or bilingual.

Second, any number of factors can help position a bilingual at a particular point on the language mode continuum. Among these we find the participant(s) (see the study described in the first section of this chapter), the situation, the form and content of the message, as well as the function of the language act. Specific research factors can also move the bilingual along the continuum, as has been shown, sometimes inadvertently, by researchers. A change in position can occur at any time as soon as the factors underlying language mode change, be it during a verbal exchange between bilinguals or, in a more controlled situation, during an experiment. In addition, the movement usually takes place unconsciously and can be quite extensive.

Third, the language mode concept can be extended to people who use three or more languages in their everyday lives. One can certainly imagine a trilingual in a monolingual, a bilingual, or a trilingual mode. And this is true for a quadrilingual who, for example, can be in a language B monolingual mode where language B is being used (it is the base language) and languages A, C, and D are not active. This same person, in another situation, can be in a quadrilingual mode where, for example, language B is the base language and languages A, C, and D are also active.

One last conceptual issue I worked on during this period concerned the Complementarity Principle which I have already mentioned. It is in a 1997 paper[10] that I gave the concept its name, and where I described it as I have done throughout this book: "Bilinguals usually acquire and use their languages for different purposes, in different domains of life, with different people. Different aspects of life require different languages." The principle has a direct impact on language proficiency. If a language is spoken in a reduced number of domains and with a limited number of people, then it will not be developed as much as a language used in more domains and with more people. In the latter case, there will be an increase in specific vocabularies, stylistic varieties, discursive and pragmatic rules, etc. It is precisely because the need and use of the languages are usually quite different that bilinguals do not develop equal and total proficiency in all their languages. This is also true for the different language skills, such as reading and writing.

I then reviewed a number of phenomena that are better understood if one takes into account the principle such as communicative competence, and the difficulties bilinguals have when translating. In a later chapter,[11] I described studies that give numerical evidence for the principle and then discussed its impact on language perception, language production, memory, and language acquisition. Finally, I argued that the principle should be taken into account when one describes language dominance. A few months after writing the chapter, I was pleased to see that the editors of the book, Carmen Silva-Corvalán and Jeanine Treffers-Daller, proposed a definition of dominance which included the principle.

Starting an academic journal

As an academic, I started reviewing papers for journals quite early on in my career. Like my peers, I would receive an invitation to give comments on the work of others and it is rare that I refused even though I always found reviewing work very demanding. It has to be done seriously and fairly, and it requires a very real understanding of each paper under consideration. I always tried to be as constructive as possible so that the author(s) could use my review to strengthen their work. I moved up one level in 1993 when Lorraine Tyler asked me to become an Associate Editor of the prestigious journal, *Language and Cognitive Processes* (now entitled *Language, Cognition and Neuroscience*). It was even more challenging but I enjoyed the work and remained an editor for four years. I then felt ready to actually help start a journal, but on bilingualism this time.

In March 1996, I went to the Netherlands to see two colleagues who also worked on bilingualism, Juergen Meisel, from the University of Hamburg, and Pieter Muysken, from the University of Amsterdam, and proposed that the three of us think about starting a journal with a cognitive slant. Up until then, all the work on bilingualism had been published in journals not specifically dedicated to those who live their lives with two or more languages and this was unfortunate. The reception they gave me was very positive and so we started brainstorming. Judith Kroll, from the Pennsylvania State University, joined us a few months later. I set about drafting a proposal which we sent to a few publishers, and after receiving a number of favorable replies, we finally decided to go with Cambridge University Press. We settled on a title, *Bilingualism: Language and Cognition,* and it was agreed that I would be the journal's first Coordinating Editor.

I remain amazed by the amount of work involved between the end of 1996 and the spring of 1998 when our journal's first issue came out. Few academics take on the task of starting a new journal and I now understand why. In a piece I wrote concerning the journal's beginnings[12] I even talk of a certain kind of "folly," which it was in a way. In addition to my duties as Coordinating Editor (I prepared 13 issues in all), I also took care of some 29 manuscripts over five years and worked with authors to get their papers ready for publication after they had been accepted by outside reviewers. Like all new journals, we made some changes over time such as increasing the length of articles and accepting special issues under the responsibility of invited editors. In December 2002, I retired from my position as editor as I felt that the six years I had spent on the journal, in addition to doing all my other academic activities, were enough and that it was on its way to being a well-established journal.

Twenty years after the first issue, the journal is doing extremely well and a short while back Patrick McCartan from the Press wrote to me: "I thought you might like to know that your creation was ranked 4th out of 179 journals in the linguistics category of the Social Science Citation Index with an Impact Factor of 2.33. What an achievement—I'm sure you're as proud as we are." His message made my day and I am indeed very proud of having been instrumental, along with my colleagues and the Press, in making this journal what it has become. May it have many good years ahead of it!

15

A life in danger

As the years went by, I remained very busy: I ran my lab which was getting continuous funding and doing good research, I took care of my Master's and Ph.D. students, I headed the University's Research Committee which oversaw all the proposals sent to the Swiss National Science Foundation, I also ran the Linguistics Institute, on a two-year rotating system, and looked after the interdepartmental Language Sciences program. I took all this in my stride and made sure I had time to spend with my family. I thought I would continue in the same rhythm until my retirement seven years later but little did I know how far from the truth that was.

A wake-up call

In the spring of 2003, I developed Raynaud's Syndrome, a condition resulting in fingers turning white and becoming numb, usually indicating an underlying problem. It quickly evolved into polymyalgia rheumatica, an inflammatory disease of the muscles and joints mainly in the top part of the body, causing pain and stiffness. I was put on a heavy dose of cortisone for several months with serious side effects and then was given shots of

A Journey in Languages and Cultures. First edition. François Grosjean.
© François Grosjean 2019. First published 2019 by Oxford University Press.

Methotrexate for a year and a half. I managed to keep up my activities, maybe with a bit less intensity, and even went to Oxford as a guest lecturer for a term in 2004 on the invitation of Kim Plunkett. It was a wonderful three months and the students I had there were all very friendly.

But then another blow struck. On a Monday morning in the fall of 2004, as I was preparing for an afternoon course, I had a heart attack in my office. I delayed going to hospital thinking it was just a stress episode, but when I did, I was immediately rushed to the University Hospital in Bern and had a coronary angioplasty and stenting procedure. It was repeated a few months later and since a blood clot was found in my heart, I was put on blood thinner in addition to having to take other heart medication. What a blow.

I started to realize that this was a turning point in my life. My family, friends, and colleagues were extremely supportive of me, and encouraged me to reduce my workload. I started turning down review requests, declined conference invitations, took time away from the office, and kept away from stressful situations. In addition, I started something I had always wanted to do—to find out about my parents' life together. I knew practically nothing about their short time together—just three and a half years. Out of this came an amazing story as well as the discovery of the man who saved my life in 1945, some 59 years before Swiss surgeons did so in 2004.

In search of my parents

I had carried with me all my life the questions I had asked myself in my youth: How had Roger and Sallie met and how had their life together been, first in England and then in France? Why did they stay with one another for such a short time? Was their love mutual, at least at first, or was it one-sided? Why did they have two children and why did neither my sister nor I ever live with either of them?

My father had died rather young in 1975—he was 55 years old—but his second wife, Jackie, was still alive and so I asked her if she had any of his documents dating back to the war. She gave me a box full, and with all the extra research I did on the side, even going to the French Air Force Archives in Dijon (France), I started putting together his story. In 2009, my mother died and a friend of hers, Alda Dapelo, phoned me to give me the news since I had been estranged from her since I was 16. Alda very kindly put aside for me family documents she found in Sallie's house in Italy, and with those, combined with the ones Jackie had given me, I had what I needed to find out about my parents' life together in England and then in France.

After Roger was demobilized from the French Air Force following the German occupation of the Vichy Free Zone in November 1942, he decided to join de Gaulle in London. To do so, he put together a very risky strategy: he made the Germans believe that if they helped him get over to England, he would send back various types of information. His Abwehr contacts in Paris told him they wanted data on aircraft, troops, weapons, instruments, and other technical matters. He would also steal a plane equipped with new navigational equipment and fly it back to German-occupied territory. The Germans helped him reach Barcelona where he went to the British Consulate and applied to be evacuated from Spain. He journeyed by train and on foot through Spain and Portugal with two other French Air Force personnel. In Lisbon, the British Embassy issued him an affidavit and organized his departure from there.

When Roger reached England in July 1943, he reported his cover story at the start of his stay at the Royal Victoria Patriotic School (London Reception Centre), an interrogation center operated by MI5 for new arrivals from continental Europe. He spent some ten days there, being debriefed, giving all the information he had, as well as names, addresses, and phone numbers. At the end of the interrogation, he was told he would be much more useful to the war effort if he agreed to be a double agent for the Security Service (MI5). This wasn't at all what he had come over for—he dreamed of doing his duty in the air with a fighter plane—but finally he agreed and became part of the Double-Cross System from August 1943 to May 1944 under the code name FIDO.

There were about forty Double-Cross agents whose task it was to send false information to the Germans primarily about the allied landings planned for June 1944. My father did so by means of letters using secret ink. By mixing correct, but unimportant, and false information, the British managed to convince the Germans that the landings would take place in the Calais/Dunkirk area. Hence they retained a number of divisions there, even after the Normandy landings had taken place, and as a consequence, numerous allied lives were saved. During that time Roger was also a member of the Free French Air Force and was given an office job. It was far too dangerous to let him fly across the Channel in case he fell into German hands and revealed what he knew. A short paper I wrote for the *International Journal of Intelligence and CounterIntelligence* relates this amazing adventure that I only learned about some twenty years after his death.[1]

As for my mother, Sallie, in addition to being a theater stage manager, she worked part-time in the Free French Club in London in 1943, and this is where she met Roger. He fell madly in love with her whereas her feelings were more ambiguous. I give evidence in a book I wrote about them[2] that Sallie was probably asked to keep Roger under surveillance by the very same service that had taken him on (MI5). They moved in together very soon after having met, and they then lived as a couple until July 1944 when he left for North Africa. Living with him was an efficient way of keeping him under surveillance, especially when the stakes were so high. It was crucial to control his movements throughout his stay in England in case he wanted to contact the Germans without referring back to MI5. This had never been his intention, but the British may not have been completely convinced of this and felt they had to keep an eye on him. As Nigel West, the well-known expert on the secret services, writes: "A single blunder, a casual indiscretion or a deliberate leak could jeopardise tens of thousands of lives on D-Day...".[3] Double agents were carefully monitored and when they moved around the country, additional surveillance was put into place.

Roger kept pushing to be sent on active flying duty but MI5 turned down his requests. They finally allowed him to go on a training course in Caistor, Lincolnshire, as this would allow the Germans to believe that he was indeed preparing to steal a plane with recent navigational equipment and fly it back to Europe. When Roger departed for his air base in mid-January, 1944, Sallie followed him a few days later, giving up her acting and theater jobs to do so. She came with a surprise: she had changed her name by Deed Poll and she was now called Sallie Henriette Grosjean. Roger was not taken aback by this extraordinary event, probably arranged by MI5. On the contrary, he was absolutely thrilled and saw this as a proof of her love.

The advantage for Sallie, of course, was that she could live with him as man and wife near his air base. I have tried since 2003 to obtain my father's file from MI5 but they have regularly refused to let me see it, using all kinds of excuses. I relate my dealings with them in another paper I wrote for the *International Journal of Intelligence and CounterIntelligence*[4] and I end it with a question: "Could the Service's reluctance to acknowledge having my father's file, and to release it, be quite simply that they do not want to admit that young English women were sometimes used for surveillance duties of agents during World War II, and that there were unwanted consequences from time to time?" In this case, two children who were to spend their youth in foster homes and then boarding schools.

The few months Roger and Sallie spent in Caistor were probably the only time both of them enjoyed each other's company, and Sallie wrote in an unpublished autobiography that Alda Dapelo had given me, "I played hide and seek with my boyfriend. He in his plane, I on my horse. The war seemed far away from the quiet countryside." She became pregnant with my sister, Brigitte, in late March 1944. When Roger was called back to London, Sallie followed him, and stayed with him until he left England in July. Sallie, along with my newborn sister, joined Roger in Paris in March 1945.

Jimmy Davis, the man who saved my life

In the documents I obtained from both Jackie and Alda Dapelo, I found notes and letters that showed that Sallie had problems adjusting to her new life in Paris, and to a husband who had practically returned to civilian life. In addition, he was no longer involved in the Double-Cross System. In August 1945, she realized that she was pregnant once again, this time with me. She thought of getting an abortion and talked about it in her auto-biography. When I read the extract in question, it left me speech-less and allowed me to understand, at least in part, her attitude towards me in my childhood. Here is what she wrote: "My second child was not desired at all, and I had desperately tried to find a way of aborting. I was too new in town and it was still illegal. One day [my husband] brought home to dinner an American soldier, Jimmy Davis, a musician. He had just finished writing a song called 'Lover Man' which became a big success. He persuaded me that it was wrong to abort. With his help, I decided to keep the baby."

For a few minutes everything around me stood still as I read my mother's words. I immediately thought back to a dinner in my father's home when I was a student in Paris, some 45 years before. When I arrived, I saw that there was a guest there who must have been in his 50s. My father introduced him to me, "This is Jimmy Davis." He then added something like, " . . . and you owe him a lot." I asked my father, "How so?" He told me that Jimmy had been friends with him and my mother when they were still together, just after the Second World War, and that Jimmy had encouraged my mother to have me, or something to that effect. It was rather vague. I don't remember much more about our dinner with Jimmy Davis and as the years went by, I almost forgot about him. From time to time, I would tell family members or close friends that an American musician had played an important role in my early life, but I was no longer sure how—not that I ever really knew. Little by little my memory of that evening faded away. I relate all of this in a 2014 *Guardian* article.[5]

That extract from my mother's autobiography allowed me to understand how Jimmy Davis had "encouraged my mother to have me." Basically, he had saved my life by convincing my mother to keep the baby she was expecting. I owed my life to someone I knew nothing about and whom I could hardly remember. So I started my search for him. It was only in November 2014 that I made some headway. I knew that he had lived in Paris in the 14th arrondissement and I went to the city hall there to obtain his death certificate. His last address was mentioned and so I walked to the building that he had lived in. I met the concierge and she introduced me to one of his friends who was still alive.

She told me a lot about Jimmy and how he would come down for dinner in his later days, showed me photos of him, and handed me the phone number of his closest friend in France. Just before leaving, she went to another room and came back with a hand-painted portrait of Jimmy by the Portuguese artist, Jacinto Luis. I had only just started admiring it when she said with a smile, "It's for you!" I was dumbfounded and asked her why. Her answer went straight to my heart: "Jimmy gave me this portrait when he was still alive. I took great care of it as I knew that someday, I would pass it on to somebody special. You are that person and you should have it!" What an amazing gift that was. A few days later, in a small Parisian café, I met Jimmy's longtime and best friend in France, a rather elderly lady who radiated kindness and warmth, and we spoke about him for three hours.

Jimmy Davis, whom I talk about in depth in the book on my parents, had an extraordinary life, professionally but also linguistically and culturally. He was born in Georgia and grew up in Gary, Illinois, and then Englewood, New Jersey. He was an extremely gifted musician and got accepted into Julliard—something very rare at the time for an African-American—where he studied piano and composition. He then tried to make a living as a songwriter and composer—it was during that time that he composed "Lover Man" with Roger (Ram) Ramirez and Jimmy Sherman—but had to do small jobs to increase his revenues, such as giving piano lessons. He enlisted in the Army when the United States entered the war, and as an active member of the NAACP, he asked to serve in an integrated unit, not a segregated one. His request was refused and he actually spent thirteen days in jail before resigning himself to joining the unit he had been assigned to.

He spent three and a half years in the Army, was appointed Warrant Officer, and made a band leader. In March 1945, he was sent to France where he stayed for only six months but this short trip marked him and would have an important impact on the rest of his life. As soon as he arrived, he wrote to his friend, Langston Hughes, that Paris was "exactly what the doctor had ordered." He returned to the US at the end of 1945 but came back for good in late 1947. As the years went by, Jimmy was one of the few American expatriate musicians from the 1940s and 1950s, along with his friend Aaron Bridgers, to remain in France. His French became very good—he composed many songs in his second language—and he interacted with both the French and the Anglo-Saxon music world.

From what I learned, Jimmy Davis had been an exceptional person, with a natural elegance, and a friendly personality. All those who knew him simply loved him. With changing tastes in music in the latter part of the last century, he had difficulties getting his work accepted, and he lived his last years very thriftily with his royalty earnings. That said, his numerous friends made sure that he was never alone, and on his eighty-second birthday, they came to celebrate him in his retirement home and show him their affection. Jimmy died in 1997 and his ashes rest in a small cemetery in the center of France, the country which welcomed him and which he adopted. There, a small plaque states, "To you, Jimmy Davis, who will remain forever our 'Lover Man', because it was so." I hope that I will be able to visit the cemetery one day and lay a rose on his grave. It would be my small gesture of love for the man who saved my life.

16
A quieter life

My autoimmune inflammatory disease lasted a number of years with all the negative consequences that went with it such as uveitis in my case. At one point, I even learned to do things with my left hand as it was less impacted than the right one. After a couple of years of trying to juggle both my illness and my career, and after having talked to my family, I decided to take early retirement. I had always enjoyed teaching and doing research, so it was a difficult decision to make but certainly the best one for me at that time. In the spring of 2006, I taught my last two courses and was happy to see that I hadn't lost too much of my teaching ability, despite the fact that my handwriting on a white board had become fairly illegible. One course received a mean of 5.45 out of 6 and the other 5.17. The comments that were added warmed my heart but also saddened me as they signaled the end of forty years of teaching.

A year later, on the last day in my lab, I wrote the following to my wife and boys, "I leave it with good memories and few regrets". I unhooked the name that had been on my door since 1987, locked the door one last time, and went to give my key back. I insisted that there be no farewell party, no goodbye drink or dinner, no speeches... basically "no fuss" as my British aunt,

A Journey in Languages and Cultures. First edition. François Grosjean.
© François Grosjean 2019. First published 2019 by Oxford University Press.

Sheila, would have said. I did receive some kind letters though, and a few presents, from my dean, the president of the university, colleagues, and even from the head of the Neuchâtel state government.

Rebuilding myself through writing

In 2004, I had approached Oxford University Press to write a book based on my lectures at Oxford that same year. I had covered some twenty-five years of my research on the bilingual person and I thought it might interest readers. I contacted John Davey and we agreed that the book, *Studying Bilinguals*,[1] would contain chapters written specifically for the book as well as reprints of my articles and chapters. John gave me a contract and I started working on the book but the submission date was pushed back several times because of my illness. I simply couldn't get rid of that inflammation and the medication I was taking was tiring me. John kept faith in me, as did Julia Steer, who had just joined Oxford University Press, and I finally finished writing the manuscript in 2007. Working on this rather long book (more than 300 pages) was a very positive experience and in many ways the therapy I had needed.

Other academic books followed. In 2011, my Parisian colleague Jean-Yves Dommergues and I published *La statistique en clair*, a very basic introduction to statistics. We had never been satisfied with the book offerings in French which we thought were far too mathematical and rather opaque for students in liberal arts and social sciences. And so, based on the introductory courses we had each taught in our respective universities, we came out with a short book that offered the basics students would need. Its success was beyond our imagination and some seven years later, as I write this, it is still in the top statistics books in French on Amazon. We dedicated it to our first statistics teacher, Harlan Lane.

Ping Li, from the Pennsylvania State University, and I then teamed up to offer a general introduction to the psycholinguistics of bilingualism. We had met in San Diego some twenty years before and he had then invited me to Hong Kong and then to Richmond on his return to the US. He had also been a subsequent Coordinating Editor of *Bilingualism: Language and Cognition*. With this book, *The Psycholinguistics of Bilingualism*,[2] we wished to offer the most important aspects of the domain in a clear, informative, and pedagogical manner, and so we teamed up with a few guest authors, experts in their own fields. We also wanted to make the issues discussed accessible to non-specialists with little exposure to the field, to give the various areas of the psycholinguistics of bilingualism equal weight, and to introduce readers to the approaches and methodology used in the field. I remain amazed that no one had opted for that title, and that it was ours to take. The book has now been out several years and is doing well.

Finally, at this level of scholarly writing, I teamed up with Krista Byers-Heinlein, of Concordia University, in Montreal, to offer *The Listening Bilingual: Speech Perception, Comprehension, and Bilingualism* which appeared in 2018.[3] We used the same model as with the book with Ping Li, that is, we wrote the majority of the chapters and let a few guest authors deal with the other chapters. It brought together in one volume the various components of spoken language processing in bilingual adults, infants, and children, and it too was destined for advanced undergraduate students as well as researchers.

For this book, as well as for the previous one with Ping Li, I spent a lot of time perusing the literature of the areas I was covering and designing chapters that told a story and that were as clear as possible. This meant reading and re-reading papers, thinking about their findings, integrating results across studies, and sometimes questioning the conclusions authors arrived at. It was a very demanding task—individual studies are not conducted with this in mind—but needed to be done so that younger researchers could quickly get an overview of the area of interest to them and then move on from there.

The last paragraph of the Introduction of *The Listening Bilingual* tells a story of life and is worth citing here: "When the preparation of a book such as this one spans a number of years, there are bound to be moments of joy and moments of sadness. We went through an especially sad moment when one of our guest authors, Lu-Feng Shi, passed away. He was a wonderful colleague to work with and he did a tremendous job despite his failing health in his last year. We will sorely miss him. However, we also went through moments of great joy during these years with, notably, the birth of a daughter, Julia, and of two grandchildren, Ismaël and Mia. They are growing up bilingual and we wish to dedicate this book to them." What is interesting is that, as I am writing this, Krista and I have still not met in person even though we worked together on this book for several years. This shows how important email is for scholarly activity, be it for research or for publications.

Nurturing bilingualism

When I thought about my bilingualism during my younger years, which I often did, I remember dreaming of general public books that would have helped me understand my life with two languages. As I wrote many years later:[4] "When I was a young student at the University of Paris coming to terms with my own bilingualism and biculturalism, I looked for a book on the subject and found only scholarly works that were rather long and difficult to read (I wasn't a linguist then). In addition, I didn't feel that they addressed the very down-to-earth issues I was interested in at that moment, nor did they answer some of my basic questions: What is bilingualism? Was I really a bilingual? Why was I suddenly having difficulties with language when things had gone smoothly until that point? (I had just returned to France after a ten-year absence.) Was I English, as my education had made me, or French, as my name and my passport indicated? Was it alright to be bicultural? These were some of the questions I was seeking answers to, and looking back over the years, I now know that many bilinguals have asked themselves the same questions."

I therefore decided to fill this gap and write the simple, basic work I had been looking for as a young man. I had two types of readers in mind. On the one hand, general readers and students, parents planning to raise or already raising bilingual children, spouses and members of extended families who interact with bilinguals, as well as colleagues and friends, and professionals who deal with bilingual children, such as teachers, psychologists, and speech therapists. On the other hand, I wanted to offer bilinguals a book about who they are, written by someone who is himself bilingual and who has been through the highs and lows of living with several languages and cultures. Many bilinguals do not consider themselves to be bilingual and are critical of their own language competence. I wanted to help them come to terms with their own reality and accept who they are—competent but different types of users of languages.

Harvard University Press, with whom I had published my first textbook on the topic a quarter of a century before, gave me a contract for *Bilingual: Life and Reality* and it came out in 2010 with a lovely cover depicting oriental lanterns at dusk.[5] It gave answers to the questions I had asked myself as a young man and tackled some fifteen myths related to bilingualism. It received very good reviews and was named CHOICE Outstanding Academic Title. It has since done well and has been translated into Italian and Arabic.

Having written this general public book in English, I turned my attention to an equivalent book in French. I have always marveled at those who write whole books in two languages,[6] but I never imagined that I would live that very experience. Once I had obtained a contract from a leading Parisian publisher, Albin Michel, I thought it would be child's play—I was fluent in both English and French, I'd been working on bilingualism for more than thirty years, and I was going to address a general public. How wrong I was though. I had to find out about bilingualism in the French-speaking world ("la Francophonie"), I had to find studies in French on various aspects of bilingualism, and I had to pay attention to aspects of bilingualism that interest the French-speaking world such as the opinions people have of their languages and of multilingualism. I also had to make sure that I had all the appropriate translation equivalents of the concepts I would be dealing with throughout the book.

But that was the easy part. The actual writing process was far harder than I had imagined. I realized that my writing style, very much influenced by my years of writing in English, simply had to become more French: written French requires far longer sentences than in English with many subordinate clauses. In addition, it usually takes on an impersonal, rather formal tone. On the level of vocabulary, written French has a tendency to use unfamiliar, rather specialized terms which must not be repeated too soon after having been used. Writers have to find ways around this either by using pronouns or finding synonyms. The problem though is that specialized words don't have exact synonyms and one is loath to use words with slightly different meanings. And, of course, I had to be careful to avoid false friends which are near homographs in English and French but with different meanings.

After a while, I found my French stride and wrote *Parler plusieurs langues: le monde des bilingues*[7] in four months. As I was doing so, my mind would often go back to bilingual authors who have written about the difficulties of writing in their two languages, or of translating their work from one language to the other. In both cases, they find that they produce very different books. When I finished this book, I knew exactly what they meant; it was very different from the one I had written on the same topic in English a few years before.

In addition to writing these two general public books, I did other things to present and defend the bilingual person: I wrote a few short texts for my website[8] (e.g. myths about bilingualism; what bilingualism is NOT; what parents want to know about bilingualism), and I started giving media interviews in writing (magazines, newspapers), for radio and on video, in both English[9] and in French.[10] I also spent quite a bit of time answering personal emails I received from people who had read me, heard me, or seen me.

One last thing I did was to start a blog, "Life as a bilingual", on *Psychology Today*.[11] When an editor, Carlin Flora, asked me in 2010 to start the blog, I asked for a few weeks to think about it. Blog posts seemed a bit short (800–1000 words) and maybe a bit too personal—as an academic, I was used to using the passive voice. But I looked around and found David Crystal's very successful blog on English linguistics. Here was a well-known academic, author, and lecturer, who had been blogging for several years and doing so most successfully. Since I was no longer teaching and I missed it, I thought it would be enjoyable to write introductory posts about various aspects of bilingualism for a general audience. So I accepted Carlin Flora's offer and became a member of the *Psychology Today* blogger group (we are currently some 850 writing on all aspects of psychology).

As with my general public books, articles, and interviews, I wanted to put to rest the many myths that surround bilingualism as well as tell the general public about findings in our field. There was also the need to reassure bilinguals about their own bilingualism and to give those involved with children (parents, educators, speech/language pathologists, etc.) some basic knowledge about growing up with two or more languages. Finally, I wanted to constitute a small on-line resource on the bilingual person, adult and child, that people can come back to at any time, free of charge.

I am a firm believer that we, researchers in language, need to inform the general public about findings in the language sciences. And since about half of the world is bilingual, and studies on bilinguals have been far less numerous than those on monolinguals until recently, we have the added duty of communicating our results on bilinguals not only to our colleagues but also to laypersons who might be interested in them. For too long this has been left to specialized journalists who simply cannot understand the field they are reporting on as well as those involved in it directly.

Writing posts for a blog is a real challenge that I took on with relish. It is far more work than it appears at first. It often requires reading several articles, contacting one or two researchers, and then writing the post so that it tells an interesting story. A finding or phenomenon must be described clearly, without too much jargon, and one needs to show the impact it has on our everyday life. My experience as a teacher, and the pleasure I found explaining things to students, guided me in this new enterprise.

After four years, Aneta Pavlenko kindly joined me on the blog, and since then we have shared the writing of posts. We have reported on strongly debated topics in the field such as the "cognitive advantages" in bilinguals found by some, but not by others, the hype around polyglots, as well as how bilinguals deal with moral dilemmas. If a domain needed specialized expertise such as the bilingual brain, we called upon experts in the field and interviewed them. We also contacted and interviewed bilingual writers and poets. As I am writing these lines, there are some 140 posts that people can read, and which we have organized by content on my website.[12] More than 1.7 million people have visited our blog, a number that astonishes us, and about which we are pleased.

Conclusion

started this book by suggesting that seen from afar, my life, both linguistic and cultural, might appear to be very ordinary... and rather French, Parisian even. Having now finished relating it, I think it is fair to say that this is not so. Yes, it did start in Paris and continued in a little French village outside that city, but then it took a number of twists and turns in four different countries and brought me in contact with a number of languages. Two were acquired sequentially and stayed, but changed their dominance at varying times (French and English) and two others were learned, used and then lost (Italian and American Sign Language). As for the four cultures I came into contact with, and lived in, they have found their place in a mosaic of cultures that characterizes me and that I am proud of.

Like in any life, there were important moments that marked it: leaving France before the age of eight for an English school in Switzerland, spending four years in a public school in England, doing my university studies in Paris, leaving for the United States as a young academic and living there for twelve years, and finally choosing to move to Switzerland instead of staying in Boston or going up to Canada. In addition, a handful of people played a crucial role in my life: Jimmy Davis in Paris who convinced my mother "to have me"; Madame Wallard, my foster mother in Villiers-Adam who saw me through my first years; a Catholic priest, Father Wood, in England who helped me during some difficult times; Antoine Culioli, a linguistics professor in Paris, who encouraged me as a fledging linguist; Harlan Lane, that young visiting professor at Vincennes who took me under his wing, invited me to America, and made me into a psycholinguist; Einar Haugen, a monument in early bilingualism research who saw my potential and encouraged it, not to mention all those who helped me along the way such as colleagues and friends. And of course, and above all, my wife and my two sons, who have always given me their support and sustained me when the going was difficult.

I firmly believe that my life as a bicultural bilingual, and my constant efforts to understand it, have influenced my research on bilingualism and biculturalism. My holistic view of bilingualism, the concept of language mode, the Complementarity Principle, what I have proposed concerning the processing of code-switches, borrowings, and interferences, and the way I characterize both the deaf bilingual and the bicultural person, among other things, would not have been what they are had I not myself experienced and been influenced by the coexistence and interaction of my own languages and cultures.

What better way to end the story of a life in languages and cultures than by evoking the future. When my first grandchild was born in 2012, I wrote him a letter which reflects in many ways what I have tried to convey in my writings, and what I dream of for the future. Here are some extracts taken from it:[1]

"My dearest little one,

One day you may read this letter written a few days after your birth. Your parents, your extended family, as well as many friends, have been celebrating your arrival among us. We have been marveling at how beautiful and how delicate you are, and we have wondered at your every move, awake or asleep.

Whilst I was admiring you during my last visit, I could not help but think that your life will be surrounded by languages and cultures . . . Being bilingual and bicultural will be a normal part of your life. You will reach the main milestones of language acquisition—babbling, first words, first phrases—at a rate similar to that of monolingual children . . . The main difference, of course, will be that you will be doing all of this in two languages—just like millions of other bilingual children—and not just one.

Of course, if one language receives more input than the other in your first years, it may become your dominant language—sounds will be isolated more quickly, more words will be acquired, and more grammatical rules will be inferred. And your dominant language may well influence your other language. But this can be corrected quickly if you change environment and your weaker language starts being used more often. It may even take over as your dominant language if the change lasts long enough.

Very quickly you will know which language to use with whom and for what. At first, you will create a strong bond between a person and his or her language . . . You will also intermingle your languages at times as a communicative strategy or to fill a linguistic need. In the latter case, you may suddenly find yourself having to say something in a language that you do not normally use for that particular domain, object, or situation. But very quickly you will learn that with people who only know one of your languages, you have to speak just their language. As the years go by, you will sometimes play with your languages. You will infringe the person-language bond and will jokingly speak to someone in the wrong language. Or you may mix your languages on purpose to raise some eyebrows.

Since your parents and grandparents have roots in different cultures, you will be introduced to them and will become bicultural. You will learn to adapt to each culture as you navigate between them and you will combine and blend aspects of these cultures. Hopefully, each of your cultures will accept you as a bicultural person and will not force you to choose one over the other. As you grow up, you will be a bridge between the cultures you belong to and you will sometimes act as an intermediary between the two.

There may be times when you are frustrated because of your bilingualism or biculturalism. Someone may make a remark about your way of saying or doing something, or may not know how to situate you. You may also struggle with a written language that you do not (yet) master well. But your parents and your extended family will be there to ease you through the difficulty and make things better.

Be proud of your linguistic and cultural roots and enjoy going back and forth between your languages and cultures. I will personally marvel at how you do so, and will help you, as best I can, to meet the challenges that you will sometimes have to face.

Welcome, my dearest little one . . . may you have a wonderful life!"

Notes

Preface and acknowledgments

1. *Bilingual: Life and Reality*. Cambridge, MA: Harvard University Press, 2010.
2. Harvard University Press, 2010.
3. Oxford University Press, 2008.

Chapter 1

1. Laurie, S. S. (1890). *Lectures on Language and Linguistic Method in the School*. Cambridge: Cambridge University Press, p. 15.

Chapter 3

1. A catalogue of their boats can be seen here: https://www.francoisgrosjean.ch/cox_and_king/
2. Grosjean, F. (2010). "Languages across the lifespan". Chapter 8 in Grosjean, F. *Bilingual: Life and Reality*. Cambridge, MA: Harvard University Press.

Chapter 4

1. Interview of François Grosjean: "Who could have imagined this kind of success for a scientific blog on bilingualism?" on Cambridge Extra: http://cup.linguistlist.org/journals/bilingualism-journals/who-could-have-imagined-this-kind-of-success-for-a-scientific-blog-on-bilingualism/ (last accessed: October 16, 2018).
2. See Grosjean, F. (2010). "Having an accent in a language". Chapter 7 in Grosjean, F. *Bilingual: Life and Reality*. Cambridge, MA: Harvard University Press.
3. See Grosjean, F. "Special bilinguals". Chapter 13 in Grosjean, F. *Bilingual: Life and Reality*. Cambridge, MA: Harvard University Press.

4. Grosjean, F. (2010). *Bilingual: Life and Reality*. Cambridge, MA: Harvard University Press, p. 245.

Chapter 5

1. Grosjean, F. (2016). "The Complementarity Principle and its impact on processing, acquisition, and dominance." In Silva-Corvalán, C. and Treffers-Daller, J. (Eds.), *Language Dominance in Bilinguals: Issues of Measurement and Operationalization*. Cambridge: Cambridge University Press.
2. Todd, O. (2005). *Carte d'identités*. Paris: Plon.
3. http://www.francoisgrosjean.ch/interview_psycholinguist_en.html (last accessed: October 16, 2018).

Chapter 6

1. Grosjean, F. (1980). "Temporal variables within and between languages." In Dechert, H. and Raupach, M. (Eds.), *Towards a Cross-Linguistic Assessment of Speech Production*. Bern: Peter Lang.

Chapter 7

1. Grosjean, F. (2010). *Bilingual: Life and Reality*. Cambridge, MA: Harvard University Press, p. 111.
2. Grosjean, F. (1980). "Spoken word recognition processes and the gating paradigm." *Perception and Psychophysics*, 28, 267–83.
3. Grosjean, F. (1985). "The recognition of words after their acoustic offset: Evidence and implications." *Perception and Psychophysics*, 38, 299–310.
4. Grosjean, F. (1983). "How long is the sentence? Prediction and prosody in the on-line processing of language." *Linguistics*, 21, 501–29.
5. Grosjean, F., Grosjean, L., and Lane, H. (1979). "The patterns of silence: Performance structures in sentence production." *Cognitive Psychology*, 11, 58–81.
6. Gee, J. and Grosjean, F. (1983). "Performance structures: A psycholinguistic and linguistic appraisal." *Cognitive Psychology*, 15, 411–58.

Chapter 8

1. Grosjean, F. (1979). "A study of timing in a manual and a spoken language: American Sign Language and English." *Journal of Psycholinguistic Research*, 8(4), 379–405.
2. See, for example, Grosjean, F. (1981). "Sign and word recognition: A first comparison." *Sign Language Studies*, 32, 195–220.
3. Grosjean, F. and Lane, H. (Eds) (1979). "La langue des signes." *Langages*, 56.
4. Lane, H. and Grosjean, F. (Eds.) (1982). *Recent Perspectives on American Sign Language*. Hillsdale, New Jersey: Lawrence Erlbaum, 275pp.
5. See, for example, Grosjean, F. (2010). "Bilingualism, biculturalism, and deafness." *International Journal of Bilingual Education and Bilingualism*, 13(2), 133–45.
6. Translations of "The right of the deaf child to grow up bilingual": http://www.francoisgrosjean.ch/the_right_en.html (last accessed: October 17, 2018).
7. See my discussion of language attrition in Chapter 3.
8. Interview with François Grosjean on Swiss television: https://www.youtube.com/watch?v=kSOaS1PF5-4 (last accessed: October 17, 2018).

Chapter 10

1. Grosjean, F. "Life as a bilingual." *Psychology Today*: https://www.psychologytoday.com/us/blog/life-bilingual (last accessed: October 18, 2018).
2. Grosjean, F. (2010). *Bilingual: Life and Reality*. Cambridge, MA: Harvard University Press, p. 217.

Chapter 11

1. Grosjean, F. (1985). "The bilingual as a competent but specific speaker-hearer." *Journal of Multilingual and Multicultural Development*, 6, 467–77.

2. Grosjean, F. (1989). "Neurolinguists, beware! The bilingual is not two monolinguals in one person." *Brain and Language*, 36, 3–15.
3. In his 1991 EUROSLA conference talk, Vivian Cook stated, "The term multi-competence makes claims about the nature of the mind that knows an L2. My starting point for this was the paper by François Grosjean called 'Neurolinguists beware! Bilinguals are not two monolinguals in one person'. In this paper Grosjean (1989) argues powerfully for the special state of the bilingual mind. A person who knows two languages is different from one who knows only one language in other respects than simply knowledge of an L2."
4. Grosjean, F. (1983). "Quelques réflexions sur le biculturalisme." *Pluriel*, 1983, 36, 81–91.
5. Grosjean, F. (2015). "Bicultural bilinguals." *International Journal of Bilingualism*, 19(5), 572–86.

Chapter 12

1. Grosjean, F., Dommergues, J.Y., Cornu, E., Guillelmon, D., and Besson, C. (1994). "The gender-marking effect in spoken word recognition." *Perception and Psychophysics*, 56(5), 590–8.
2. For more information on these studies, see Chapter 3 of Grosjean, F. (2008). *Studying Bilinguals*. Oxford: Oxford University Press.
3. I talk about whether a first language can be totally forgotten, and describe studies aimed at answering the question, on my blog, "Life as a bilingual," *Psychology Today*, https://www.psychologytoday.com/us/blog/life-bilingual (last accessed: October 18, 2018).
4. A number of interviews can be found here: https://www.francoisgrosjean.ch/interviews_en.html (last accessed: October 18, 2018).
5. Grosjean, F. (2018). "America, we care about you!" OpEd in *Le Temps*, January 23: https://www.letemps.ch/opinions/america-we-care-about-you (last accessed: October 18, 2018).

Chapter 13

1. Among the publications that emanated from this research, see for example: Cornu, E., Kübler, N., Bodmer, F., Grosjean, F., Grosjean, L., Léwy, N., Tschichold, C., and Tschumi, C. (1996). "Prototype of a second language writing tool for French speakers writing in English." *Natural Language Engineering*, 2(3), 211–28.
2. See, for example, Miller, J. and Grosjean, F. (1997). "Dialect effects in vowel perception: The role of temporal information in French." *Language and Speech*, 40(3), 277–88.

Chapter 14

1. Grosjean, F. (1997). "Processing mixed language: Issues, findings and models." In de Groot, A. and Kroll, J. (Eds.). *Tutorials in Bilingualism: Psycholinguistic Perspectives*. Mahwah, NJ: LEA, 1997.
2. Grosjean, F. and Miller, J. (1994). "Going in and out of languages: An example of bilingual flexibility." *Psychological Science*, 5(4), 201–6.
3. Guillelmon, D. and Grosjean, F. (2001). "The gender marking effect in spoken word recognition: The case of bilinguals." *Memory and Cognition*, 29(3), 503–11.
4. Soares, C. and Grosjean, F. (1984). "Bilinguals in a monolingual and a bilingual speech mode: The effect on lexical access." *Memory and Cognition*, 12(4), 380–6.
5. Grosjean, F. (1988). "Exploring the recognition of guest words in bilingual speech." *Language and Cognitive Processes*, 3(3), 233–74.
6. Léwy, N. and Grosjean, F. (2008). "The Léwy and Grosjean BI-MOLA model." Chapter 11 of Grosjean, F. (2008). *Studying Bilinguals*, pp. 201–10. Oxford/New York: Oxford University Press.
7. Grosjean, F. (1998). "Studying bilinguals: Methodological and conceptual issues." *Bilingualism: Language and Cognition*, 1, 131–49.
8. Cutler, A., Mehler, J., Norris, D., and Segui, J. (1992). "The monolingual nature of speech segmentation by bilinguals." *Cognitive Psychology*, 24, 381–410.

9. Grosjean, F. (2001). "The bilingual's language modes." In Nicol, J. (Ed.). *One Mind, Two Languages: Bilingual Language Processing* (pp. 1–22). Oxford: Blackwell.

10. Grosjean, F. (1997). "The bilingual individual." *Interpreting*, 2(1/2), 163–87.

11. Grosjean, F. (2016). "The Complementarity Principle and its impact on processing, acquisition, and dominance." In C. Silva-Corvalán and J. Treffers-Daller (Eds.), *Language Dominance in Bilinguals: Issues of Measurement and Operationalization.* Cambridge: Cambridge University Press.

12. Grosjean, F. (2007). "Starting BLC: 1996–1998." *Bilingualism: Language and Cognition*, 10(1), 3–6.

Chapter 15

1. Grosjean, F. (2010). "FIDO: French pilot and Security Service double agent malgré lui." *International Journal of Intelligence and CounterIntelligence*, 23(2): 337–52.

2. Grosjean, F. (2016). *A la recherche de Roger et Sallie.* Hauterive, Switzerland: Editions Attinger. (The English version is as yet unpublished).

3. Quote from the Introduction of Liddell, G. (2005). *The Guy Liddell Diaries.* Vol. II: 1942–1945. Edited by Nigel West. Abingdon, England.

4. Grosjean, F. (2014). "The Security Service and a family's right to know." *International Journal of Intelligence and CounterIntelligence*, 27(2): 428–30.

5. Grosjean, F. (2014). "The American jazz musician who saved my life." *The Guardian*, Saturday, December 6. Available at: https://www.theguardian.com/lifeandstyle/2014/dec/06/the-american-jazz-musician-who-saved-my-life (last accessed: October 19, 2018).

Chapter 16

1. Grosjean, F. (2008). *Studying Bilinguals*. Oxford: Oxford University Press.
2. Grosjean, F. and Li, P. (2013). *The Psycholinguistics of Bilingualism*. Malden, MA and Oxford: Wiley-Blackwell.
3. Grosjean, F. and Byers-Heinlein, K. (2018). *The Listening Bilingual: Speech Perception, Comprehension, and Bilingualism*. Hoboken, NJ: Wiley.
4. Extract from the Introduction to Grosjean, F. (2010). *Bilingual: Life and Reality*. Cambridge, MA: Harvard University Press.
5. Grosjean, F. (2010). *Bilingual: Life and Reality*. Cambridge, MA: Harvard University Press.
6. See Grosjean, F. (2010). "Bilingual writers", Chapter 12 in Grosjean, F. *Bilingual: Life and Reality*. Cambridge, MA: Harvard University Press.
7. Grosjean, F. (2015). *Parler plusieurs langues: le monde des bilingues*. Paris: Albin Michel.
8. https://www.francoisgrosjean.ch/index.html (last accessed: October 19, 2018).
9. https://www.francoisgrosjean.ch/interviews_en.html
10. https://www.francoisgrosjean.ch/interviews_fr.html
11. https://www.psychologytoday.com/us/blog/life-bilingual (last accessed: October 19, 2018).
12. https://www.francoisgrosjean.ch/blog_en.html

Conclusion

1. https://www.psychologytoday.com/intl/blog/life-bilingual/201211/born-be-bilingual (last accessed: October 19, 2018).

Index

Index

adapts to American culture 68–70, 72–3
and culture shock 27–9, 38–9, 65–6
and his bicultural identity 39–41, 56, 120–1
becomes bicultural 20–2
finally accepts his Anglo-Saxon side 79
misses the United States 106, 132
stranger in his own country 38–9, 43–4

Grosjean, François, on his own bilingualism:
asked to be a linguistic informant 46
becomes bilingual 17–18
change of language dominance 38, 113, 116, 177
first contact with English 15
monolingual years 9–16
why not brought up bilingual from birth 5–6
see also Grosjean, François, languages

Grosjean, François, on the bilingualism of his family:
helping his children settle in Switzerland 134–5
his first son shifts over to English 70–1, 99–100
keeping the children's bilingualism alive back in the US 107–9
letter to his first grandchild 178–80
the children's contact with the French-speaking world 102
the children start acquiring French naturally 102–5
their language status after one year abroad 107

see also Grosjean, Cyril; Grosjean, Lysiane; Grosjean, Pierre

Grosjean, François, perception of the countries he lived in:
England 27–8
France 39, 69
Switzerland 105–6, 135–7
United States 65–6, 68–70, 131–2

Grosjean, François, research topics:
bilingualism of the deaf 85–90
bilinguals in Paris 48–50
change of first language in contact with second language 125–7
Complementarity Principle 37–8, 112, 114–15, 154–5, 178
holistic view of bilingualism 114–17; *see also* bilingualism, holistic view of
language mode in bilinguals 115, 123–4, 143–4, 150, 152–3
language processing in bilinguals 124–5, 143–50; *see also* bilingualism, perception studies; bilingualism, production studies
natural language processing 138–9
oral language tests for aphasic patients 139
prosodic structure 125
prosody 78, 125
research methodology in bilingualism research 150–2
sign language processing 82–3
spoken word recognition in bilinguals 124–5, 146–7, 148–9
spoken word recognition in monolinguals 76, 125, 140
temporal variables (rate and pausing) 61–2, 125

Index

Index

Index